Rozanne Hawksley

Mary Schoeser

Ruthin Craft Centre / Lund Humphries

Author
Mary Schoeser

Editor
June Hill

Photography
Dewi Tannatt Lloyd
(unless stated)

Design
Lawn
www.lawncreative.co.uk

Print
Graphicom, Italy

ISBN 978-1-84822-026-3

Published by
Ruthin Craft Centre
The Centre for the Applied Arts,
Park Road, Ruthin, Denbighshire,
North Wales LL15 1BB
Tel: +44 (0)1824 704774
www.ruthincraftcentre.org.uk

in association with

Lund Humphries
Wey Court East,
Union Road, Farnham,
Surrey GU9 7PT

and

Lund Humphries
Suite 420, 101 Cherry Street,
Burlington VT 05401-4405 USA

Lund Humphries is part of Ashgate Publishing
www.lundhumphries.com

British Library Cataloguing-in-Publication Data
A catalogue record for this book is available from the British Library

Library of Congress Control Number: 2009920487

COVER, BACK COVER AND RIGHT *Pale Armistice*, 1991. Photograph by Damon Cleary,
courtesy of the Imperial War Museum.

Rozanne Hawksley

Offerings

One has to be so careful these days, 2004.

Et ne non inducas (And lead us not), 1987–89, detail.

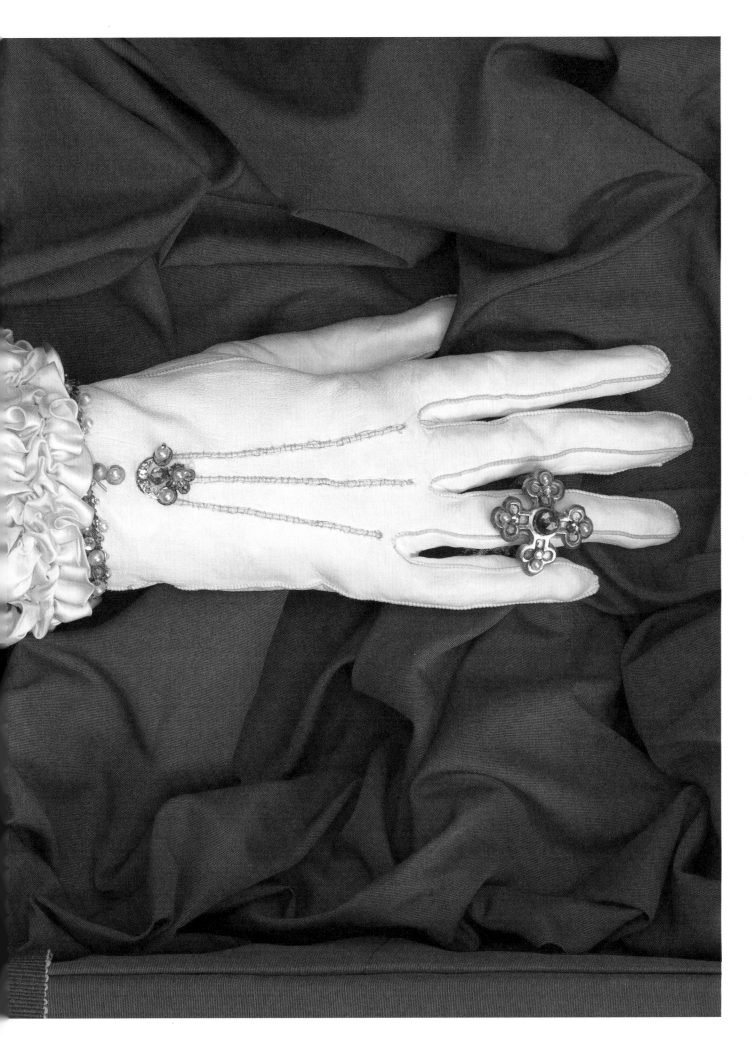

'*...a treaty will be signed some time today*', installation, 1997, as shown at the Mission Gallery. Photographs by Nicola O'Neill.

PREFACE

The 1988 *Subversive Stitch* exhibition at Manchester's Cornerhouse Gallery, is today recognised as a seminal point in the history of contemporary textile practice. Rozanne Hawksley was one of its stars. Two decades on, she is today known as one of the UK's great textile art innovators, whose work lies far beyond simple categories. Her best known piece, *Pale Armistice*, is now in the permanent collection of the Imperial War Museum, and has been widely exhibited. Her installation, *...a treaty will be signed sometime today*, was originally devised in 1997 for the Mission Gallery in Swansea, then toured the UK and Ireland as part of the 2000 Knitting and Stitching Show. In common with other pieces, both railed against the iniquity of those who conspire to wage war, but in very different ways. *Pale Armistice* was a quiet, reflective wreath made from white and cream gloves and imparts its message with subtle dignity. *Treaty* is a visceral tableau of bones, blood and rage.

A recent piece, *The Seamstress and the Sea*, was inspired by the life experience of her grandmother, an outworker for one of the (then many) naval tailors in Portsmouth. It recounts a sailor's life through her piecework on hundreds of collars, and subtly draws on the realities of naval life at that time, such as the suture patterns a surgeon would have used to close wounds. The resulting tableau charts the passage of time and the arc of a sailor's life, from the making of his collar to his shroud, and final resting place deep in the ocean. Assembled before the onlooker they form a quiet altar, a contemporary relic, a contemplative shrine to the perils of life at sea, and a celebration of the invisible seamstresses and the sailors who were buried anonymously at sea in the garments they made.

Rich in allegorical references, her work charts an odyssey encompassing the universal and intensely personal. Recurrent themes are the fragility of the human condition and the immorality of war. There is fascination with revealing the darker, macabre even, side of existence, with reinterpreting centuries-old *memento mori*, but within a unique and life-affirming embrace. She mistrusts the glib certainty of authority, and feels profound rage against loss and injustice. She questions Catholicism, yet retains a love of ritual. These tensions underpin her creativity. They are manifest throughout her work, and in her messages and strategies to engage and draw us in – a combination of opulence, horror, 'decadence' and theatre. All are vehicles for her messages, which can be as subtle as faint music from long ago, or can strike with visceral power. Any study of her work will stimulate, provoke, inspire and mystify.[1]

Philip Hughes, Director,
Ruthin Craft Centre

Aimez-vous le big Mac?, 2008.

Pale Armistice, 1991. Photograph by Damon Cleary, courtesy of the Imperial War Museum.

FOREWORD

Her loveliest of wreaths, *Pale Armistice* –
composed from a multitude of whitish
gloves, lain gently over one another – was
my first encounter with Rozanne Hawksley's
work. I came across it unexpectedly in
the Imperial War Museum, and can well
remember standing stock-still before it
for a long time, mesmerized by its simple
beauty. It is an extraordinary exhibit in
that vast place devoted to war.

Attempting subsequently to analyse
why her work had affected me so deeply,
I puzzled over how it was that the effect
continued long afterwards in memory.
What caught me unawares was its gentle
mix of wit and sorrow, beauty and sadness,
tenderness and mischief. Whoever had
created it, I knew, understood love and loss,
and was an adept at bestowing comfort,
too, directly and deep into the human heart.

The wreaths of official remembrance
represent a well-established stable
compound of metaphorical meanings:
evergreens are insignia of both memory
and of grief (always green) and poppies
represent both blood spilled and spiritual
resurrection after carnage. *Pale Armistice*
represents a moving and highly effective
transmutation of the green and red wreath
of official ceremonial, translating it into
something altogether more modest and
more tender: substituting the pale shades
of real men's and women's gloves for the
regimented fierce colours and shiny surfaces
of evergreen foliage and false poppies.

The reality and informality of the
gloves in Rozanne Hawksley's sculpture,
their tints and textured softness, allows
them to serve as perfect analogues for real
human hands, emphasizing human variety,
human corporeality and human touch,
in a never-ending cycle of comfort.

Pale Armistice is a triumph of a subversive
surrealism, simultaneously bearing delight
and gravity; and it is, too, a feminist
meditation on memorialization, not only
of those killed in war, but of its damaged
and bereaved survivors.

Since then, I have discovered others
who love Rozanne Hawksley's compassionate
art. A friend (the artist Jane Wildgoose)
alerted me when *The Seamstress and the Sea*
was on exhibition at HMS Belfast, and
I made the journey to that rather harsh
and bleak floating environment, in the
winter of 2006. It was a sort of pilgrimage
of admiration without knowing what
to expect. I was not disappointed.

The small windowless room inside
the ship in which the exhibition was
installed had been transformed by means
of an abundance of creamy linen fabric,
from an unforgiving metal box to a soft
and warm palace of maiden thought. Alice
Hunter, the 'Seamstress' of the exhibition's
title, was Rozanne Hawksley's grandmother.
In the first half of the 20th century, she had
made a thin living skilfully sewing the
complex square collars traditionally worn
by sailors of the Royal Navy. The intimate
relationship between fabric and skin, sewing
and suturing, life and death, love and
descent, was demonstrated in the dexterous
and nurturative manual skills handed down
through the female side of her family.

I have awaited this important
retrospective exhibition of Rozanne
Hawksley's work with considerable
anticipation. There will be many like me
who will travel far to see her works of art,
so delicate in themselves, so tentatively bold,
and so brimming with humanity.

Dr Ruth Richardson

Queen of Spades, 2008.

Our Lady of the Seven Sorrows, 2000–02, 33cm high.

Rozanne Hawksley
Offerings

Mary Schoeser

A Mitre for the Bishop of London, 1997–98, detail. Photograph by Bob Pullen.

THE SEAMSTRESS AND THE SEA

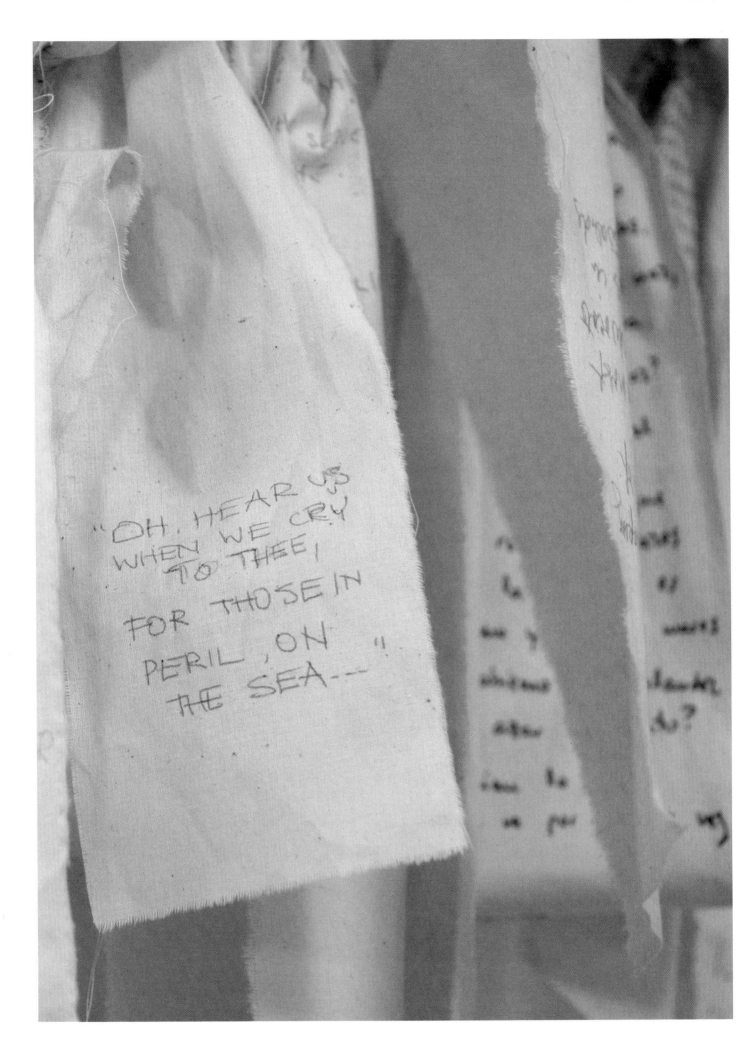

Rozanne Hawksley's compelling installation, *The Seamstress and the Sea*, evolved from a commission to exhibit as one of eleven artists in *Sample*, a show touring the UK and the Netherlands from August 2003 until May 2004. Soon afterwards included with work by five others in *Of Sea and Stars*, at the Mission Gallery, Swansea, the receipt of an Arts Council of Wales grant gave her the opportunity to develop her concept into a solo show, which opened in October 2006 on *HMS Belfast*, the Thames-moored battle cruiser owned by the Imperial War Museum. In the following year it was exhibited for five months at Portsmouth City Museum. Modified and expanded with each showing, the installation typifies the slow gestation of much of Rozanne's work. It began by drawing upon her own family background and her experiences as a child growing up in Portsmouth, where she was born in February 1931. In the end, however, it became a memorial to hundreds of men and women who served or died at sea. As a work of art, it is thus both autobiographical and universal, a cohesion of vividly recalled individual memories – hers and others' – and observations about war, women's work, and rank, whether social or military. In its expression of the personal and the personification, the installation reflects a recurrent quality in Rozanne's work, making its closer study a fitting introduction to her methods and artistic intentions.

The seamstress to whom the title refers is Alice Hunter, Rozanne's maternal grandmother. The widow Alice sewed sailor's collars for a living from World War I until her death during World War II, supporting six children by working from home for Bourne's, a naval tailor and outfitters in Queen Street, Portsmouth. Around a corner was Hay Street, its small terraced houses lining a narrow cobbled lane close to the main dockyard gate. Life for the Hunters at No.10 was hard but not impossibly so. Rozanne recalls the decency, humour and respect for themselves and others, the latter including the Bournes, who also employed her mother's youngest sister, Winnie, behind the counter: 'without their care and good hearts... the little Hunter family, fatherless, would have been broken up and sent to the workhouse – with dreaded consequence.' Nevertheless, outside the front door was a district named as one of the worst slums in Britain prior to World War I; it was little better during the 1920s and '30s, with its crowded poverty and ill health. There also lived the sister of a friend of her mother's, with her unwell unemployed husband and two children in one room and a bit of a passage in a dark basement, which Rozanne remembers visiting when she was about four. 'The young mother was lying on her side on a double bed; I can't remember any sheets but worn lino on the floor... hardly any furniture... like a Cruickshank illustration of Dickensian poor. God knows how they washed or cooked, or even ate, but this woman was very ill and I remember the smell of illness and poverty.'[1]

Rozanne's own family, the Pibworths, lived not far away in a rented maisonette, but in more comfortable circumstances.

PREVIOUS *Alice's World*, drawing on canvas, 2006, detail. A series of superimposed maps, from Fleet where Alice Hunter was born to the world within which her collars' wearers served. The photograph shows Rozanne as a young child with her grandmother, Alice Hunter, and mother, Wendy Pibworth (foreground).

OPPOSITE *In Memoriam*, 2006–07, detail from the streamers inscribed by visitors to *The Seamstress and the Sea* on board HMS Belfast. Photograph by Dil Bannerjee, courtesy of the Imperial War Museum.

LEFT The Imperial War Museum's poster for *The Seamstress and the Sea*, 2006.

Hers was a neighbourhood appearing 'as certainly "better off" and where, if poverty existed, it was hidden.' Her father, Arthur Henry, always known as Turo, was a bank clerk; his only sister, Auntie Ella, was a Queen Alexandra matron who nursed around the world, while his five brothers included several with naval connections, ranging from Uncle Leonard's work in the dockyards to Uncle Jack's frequent deployment in Scotland, as a naval officer. Roz's paternal grandfather had also been a naval officer. However, Rozanne hardly ever saw her father's relatives; to her they were like shadows, kept at arms length by her father. She conjectures that it was due, perhaps, to his snobbishness, his discomfort with his own kin resulting from the fact that, as Rozanne often heard

said, 'Father married lower-deck.' His wife Wendy, one of Alice Hunter's children (christened Alice Lillian Rose, but called Wendy after the character in *Peter Pan*), was indeed from a different background. Nevertheless, she did not work once she married. While Rozanne's grandmother's stitching was utilitarian, her mother and aunt's needlework was mostly decorative. 'Everybody embroidered – chairbacks, tray cloths, tea cosies – and we went to the Bon Marché to get linen crash.' During the 1930s these little acts of beauty were tiny barriers against the worst of the Depression, an event that Rozanne feels shaped her, but also had an equal impact on many others: 'people of my age then were the off-spring of parents who worked terribly hard for very little.

ABOVE *Alice & Rozanne*, photo-montage, 2006.
Photograph by Philip Clarke.

My father regretted all his life he'd left the security of the Indian Army and worked in a bank.' Her mother, on the other hand, is remembered for her sense of fun, and in brief moments of nostalgia, while working on *The Seamstress and the Sea*, Rozanne recalled her close bond with her mother, to which she attributes her sense of 'how lovely the world was and how lucky I was to be a happy child then.'

Despite her secure home life, being in a garrison town with a naval base and many Service hospitals meant the same environment was peopled with men who had been badly wounded. In bright blue suits and bright red ties, they were on crutches or in wheelchairs or 'invalid carriages', the latter frightening to the young Rozanne; 'those long, long prams... almost like coffins with a hood on two wheels and... pushed like a handcart.' Particularly upsetting was a man who had lost both legs. 'He had an old "pram" containing a horned gramophone on which he played one of his three-or-so wax records – a sad sound in itself – and an upturned hat as a receptacle for donated coins.' Much later her mother confessed that more than a few hours were spent avoiding him and 'when we walked back on nice days we had to go down a side road and then up another one so that I would not burst into tears with sorrow for this "poor man with horses hooves"...'. Such experiences remain fundamental to Rozanne's world view, and her indignation rises even today. When recently confronted with the way Service people are treated she could not help but comment, 'I mean honestly, talk about sending them out and not protecting them and respecting them – it really is dreadful!' Such experiences also reflected her youthful understanding of the losses her own family had suffered due to war. Among her father's five brothers was Uncle Bert, who had lost a leg in 1916 at the Battle of the Somme, and whose noisy gait had aroused her curiosity as a child. Far less innocent to the impact of such conflicts by the end of World War II, she recalls her godmother's son, Jimmy, first as a naughty little boy at Portsmouth Grammar, aged eleven on her fifth birthday, and then, after over three years as a prisoner of war in the Far East and aged then over 21, 'like a skeleton... but his uniform was immaculate and as he came through the gate the sun shone off his Sam Browne belt.' The POW camp had been Changi in Singapore, where fewer than ten percent of prisoners survived; the young man was James Clavell, and his story became the 1962 bestseller, *King Rat.*

Grandma Alice, too, knew such losses, for it was a Highland soldier who had won her heart while she served as a lady's maid in Dorset, and it was this same William Hunter whom she had married and lost to the flu epidemic that killed six million people as it swept through Europe during the final months of World War I. At No.10 Hay Street, however, Rozanne found a fascinating environment. Her grandmother long since had been promoted to making up the entire collar, as opposed to the sewing of the three stripes only.

In her statement for the *HMS Belfast* installation, she recounts her fascination with the speed of her grandmother's treadle sewing machine and the strong memories of Alice at work in the little back room: 'great piles of cloth; the sound of her needle drawing the waxed thread through the tough cloth and a particular noise that was her thimble against the eye of her needle; of her singing sad and jolly songs of the First World War as she sewed; "There's a long, long trail a-winding" and so often the Regimental March of the Royal Marines.' Other sounds intermingled: 'The sound of the thick fabric being "turned-through" after stitching – making a loud crack. It seemed like magic that the almost finished collar appeared.'

Rozanne was 12 or 13 when her grandmother died, and the opportunity to honour her by doing research into her life and work came with *Sample*, an Embroiderers' Guild exhibition that invited submissions from established artists who wished to broaden their field of practice. She 'set herself the challenge of exploring stitch as the subject itself, the purely utilitarian stitch – stitch for specific needs, its historic and social significance, using as a starting point a very personal history...'.[2] The need for a proposal initially stumped her. 'I don't really work like that, I can't foresee it.' Knowing that 'somewhere would be a replica of a collar... I had no idea apart from the sort of snatches of patchwork that shot in and out of my mind like a mosquito... so I did something which I don't do normally: I started to draw.' Not that drawing itself was unusual, far from it. The unusual point was to *start* with a drawing to get an idea. 'I normally pick up several feelings over several months, maybe years, and suddenly they start to form a whole, then I make written notes.' But in this case, 'I began to get in my mind that this would not necessarily be me

remembering it all but certainly a great part of it would be based on one sailor... unwounded but remembering a ship being torpedoed and some of his crew. That is how it started. It did itself really.'

Crediting her muse, talking of how a piece reveals itself, describing a kind of unease that makes it imperative to begin creating, all these are aspects of the same impulse in the artist to credit her work as having an existence entirely separate from herself. It is this quality that transforms even her most personal pieces into transcendental observations, deriving their power from an abstract ubiquity, a complete acceptance and understanding of the ordinary that, once distilled, imbues the finished article with something like a sense of inevitability. In the case of *The Seamstress and the Sea*, the 'ordinary' resided in the sailors' collars, made in the hundreds of thousands by women like Alice Hunter but, today, extremely rare. This is because the seaman's uniform, unlike those for officers, remained the property of the Royal Navy and 'unless the man was killed and/or buried at sea, his kit was handed in and officially disposed of – the cloth being sold on and turned into "shoddy".

LEFT *For Alice Hunter*, 2003. This assemblage of sailor's collar with seamstress's sewing equipment includes items from as near Alice's time as possible, including Alice's own ball of tailor's wax. Photograph by Philip Clarke.

ABOVE *'We Jolly Sailor Boys': Remembering*, pencil and pastel on paper, 2003.

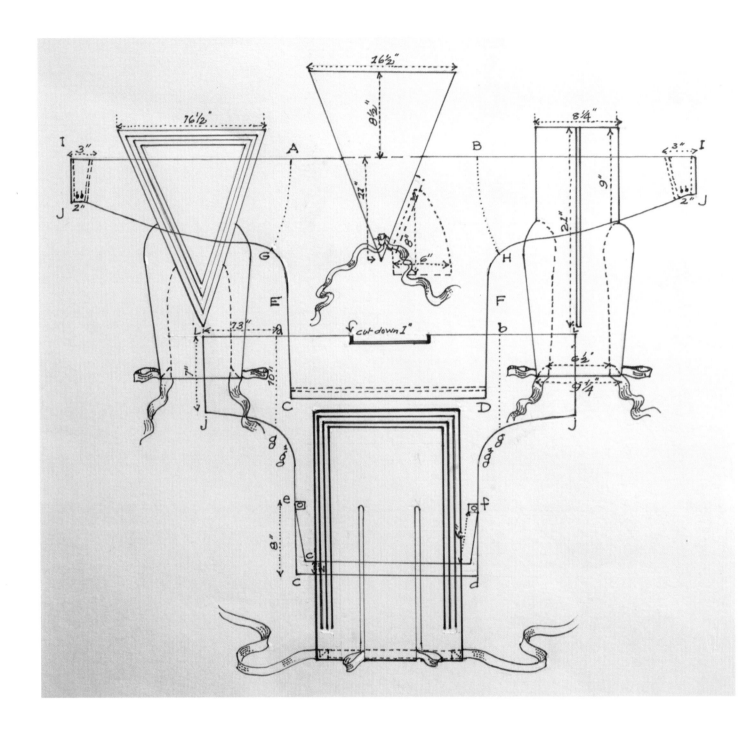

ABOVE *Reconstructed Patterns*, drawings on canvas, 2003. These diagrams show the evolution of the collars worn by sailors upto the regulation on which Alice Hunter worked. The top image records earlier collars and the jerkin over which they would have been worn. The lower drawing is the shape Alice would have made, superimposed over the sailor's shirt.

RIGHT *Finished Collar in Calico*, 2003. Worn under the jerkin and over the shirt. Photograph by Philip Clarke.

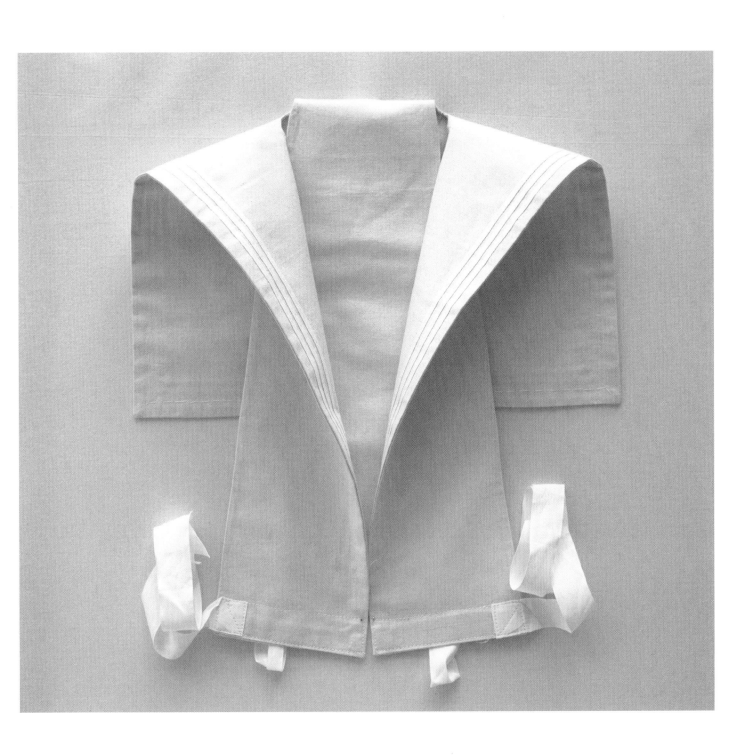

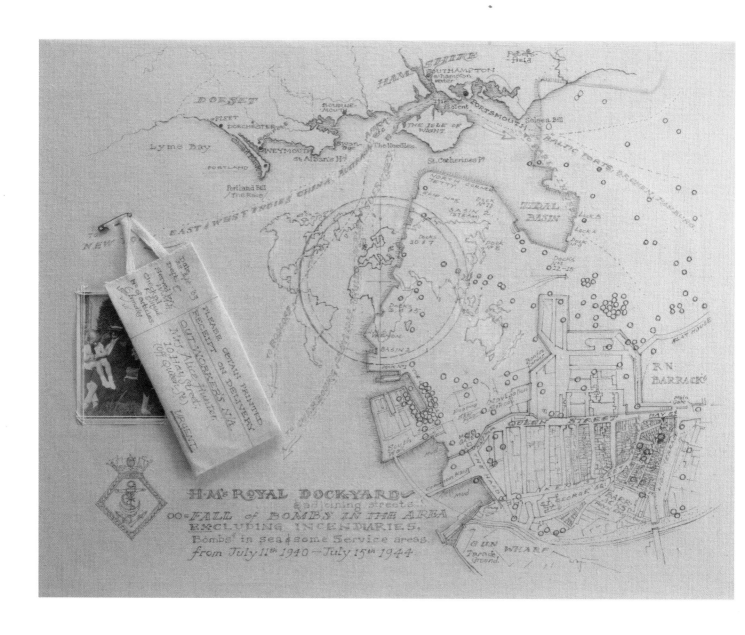

ABOVE *Alice's World*, drawing on canvas, 2006. A large map of Portsmouth HM Dockyard and the area around it where Alice lived and worked, is superimposed over a map of the world within which her collars' wearers served.

Determined to begin by making a replica collar, her enquiries at the Greenwich Naval Museum located some information on regulation sizes but, to her surprise, no knowledge that women out-workers made the collars or how they were made.

Undeterred, Rozanne's visualisation of the possible work began to germinate, and she sought a balance between her emotional and intellectual responses to her topic in a trip to Portsmouth, where in the Royal Naval Museum she had located two sailors' collars, 'both very worn and faded but with the men's initials still visible on the reverse.' Aware of their scarcity, she recalls being 'extraordinarily moved when I handled the two collars – because of the makers and the men who wore them.' Elaborating on this topic, she continues: 'two collars only and they thought that Grandma probably made them, because they were made locally and the rating had written his initials on the back as was usual, in indelible pencil, and it was very touching when you know that the last inch that holds the collar together, in place, so that it sits right for each individual... is done by the sailor himself using his little "hussif"; his set of needles and threads.' Next she went to the Naval Research Library, where one nineteenth century book that had survived the bombing raids preserved in words and diagrams the rules and regulations surrounding naval uniforms, which only began to be codified in the 1830s. The collars as made by Alice Hunter remained unchanged in their form from about the 1880s into the mid-1950s, yet no patterns survived. These she was to work out for herself. 'So this is how I proceeded, by drawing the collar on paper, making a pattern and then machining the various tapes onto where I thought they should go, because it is quite complicated. ...but eventually I did find a way...'. Ever aware of the forgotten hands of many out-workers such as her grandmother, to this she adds, 'and of course, these women were doing hundreds at a time...'.

Finally, she walked the ramparts of old Portsmouth, 'the Sally Port, past the shell of the Garrison church, into the cathedral where my parents were married (their local parish church) and I was christened.' This brought back other memories too: 'My father used to take me to the Garrison church some Sundays, and I can see [the Royal Marines] now; they looked like giants with their white huge gauntlets on and their white pith helmets with a spike on top. Oh, I did want one so desperately and I went on and on and "all I want for Christmas is an RM helmet" ...maybe my father had to bribe someone to get it [or] it was a pretend one, [but] it was *big*.' Explaining further that in the Royal Marines the drummer wore a leopard skin with the head hanging down his back, she envisions 'its spotty beautiful fur with its mouth in a snarl and its glass eyes and its great paws and it was always lying on a beautiful red, I suppose it was broadcloth... which looked as though the animal was lying on a bright red rug – I never thought that it might have been blood but I would now, wouldn't I?'

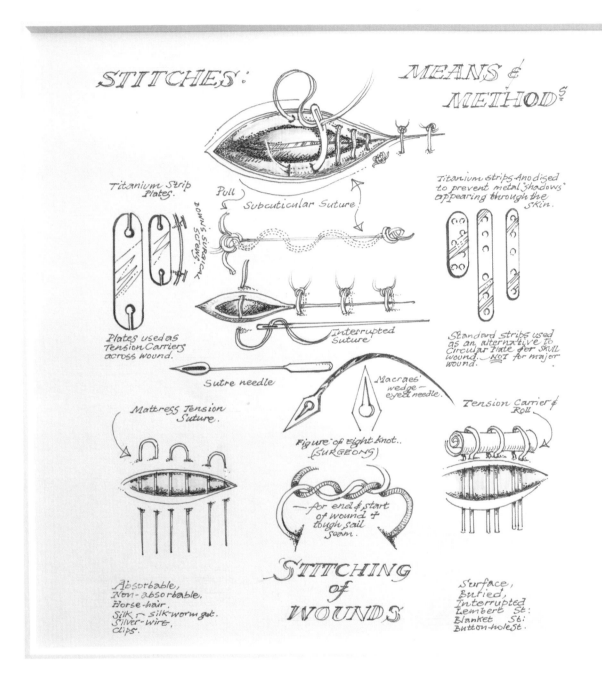

STITCHES: *MEANS &
METHODs*

Titanium Strip
Plates.

Pull

Subcuticular Suture.

Titanium strips Anodised
to prevent metal "shadows"
appearing through the
skin.

DOWNS SURGICAL SCREWS.

Plates used as
Tension Carriers
across wound.

Interrupted
Suture

Standard strips used
as an alternative to
Circular Plate for SKULL
wound. NOT for major
wound.

Sutre needle

Macraes'
wedge-
eyed needle.

Mattress Tension
Suture.

Figure of eight knot..
(SURGEONS)

Tension Carrier &
Roll

for end & start
of wound &
tough sail
seam.

*STITCHING
of
WOUNDS*

Absorbable,
Non-absorbable,
Horse-hair.
Silk ~ silk-worm gut.
Silver-wire,
Clips.

Surface,
Buried,
Interrupted
Lembert St:
Blanket St:
Button-hole st.

ABOVE *Stitches: Means & Methods & Stitching
of Wounds*, drawing on paper, 2003.

RIGHT *Surgeon's Equipment*, 2003, detail. The skull shows
the imagined treatment of a head wound, monochromatic
except for the threads of red silk floss.

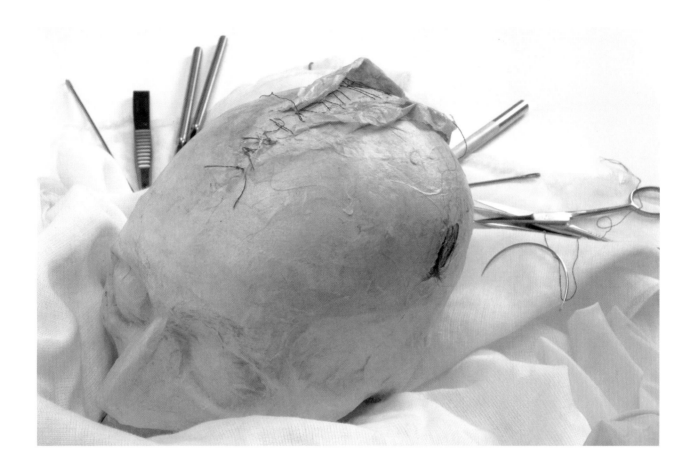

Such collisions of joyful and sorrowful memories filled her mind as she walked amid the ghostly remnants of her grandmother's neighbourhood, working out which of two little cobbled streets was Hay Street, by its little slope downwards to the corner where the ice-cream makers had kept their horse and cart. She realised as she moved on to the Museums and Record Office that 'I actually found *myself* by looking; it was that finding that moved me.' Then, in the record office, she recalled the house number, a number not spoken for decades, and was shown a map of the area made in the late 1940s, covered with red dots each representing a bomb site. 'There were seven red dots on little Hay Street.' The horror of war was embedded in these obliterating dots, and

emotionally erased through her creation of *Alice's World*, a drawing on canvas charting the area around Portsmouth's Dockyard and Naval Base and its connections that had once stretched around the world.

Out of this limited cash of information and wealth of sensory stimulation came a range of objects bound together by their connection to stitching: a collage of sewing paraphernalia that might have been Alice's, reconstructed collar patterns, a 'toile' or canvas prototype collar and, in the same material, a body bag intended for a sailor's burial at sea. This sailor is depicted in that pivotal initial pencil drawing, in which the surviving seaman is haunted by a vision of his shipmates around a wounded man, attended by the skeleton of Death.

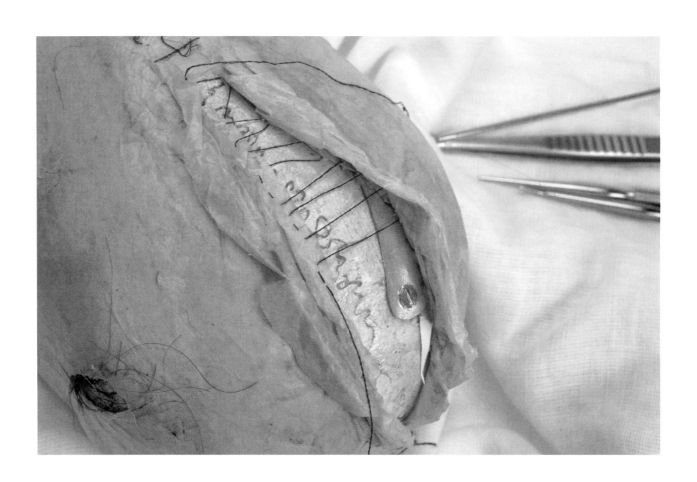

The installation thus turns subtlety into the tale of a seaman's life, from the making of his collar to his shroud, the imagined soul commemorated in *Memorial Wreath*, made with sailor's silk as worn with the collar when in No.1 Rig. Yet equally evident is Rozanne's curiosity, her leap of imagination from seamstress's needle to surgeon's needle, represented by another collage, this time of a ship's surgeon's equipment, and explained in *Stitches: Means & Methods*, a drawing depicting surgical needles and stitches. She had discovered these were essentially the same as domestic needles and stitches through research at the Wellcome Trust Library, where a volume on head wounds showed the very early use of protective plates of titanium, chosen for its lightness and because it didn't show through the skin. 'So that did itself too... there is the top of the skull which I made with a plastic one and painted very carefully, and then put false layers of skin over it very very tight, very very fine, very very thin. And then stitched that in red floss silk...'. What kept Alice and her family alive on shore, one sees, were the same needles, threads and hand-motions that might keep a sailor alive at sea.

In its final form, *The Seamstress and the Sea* is a treble memorial. The first, of course, is to Alice Hunter, who not only represents out-workers generally, but Rozanne's introduction to the idea that one could live by stitching. Commemorated further by photographs and period postcards of Portsmouth, Alice also typifies the affectionate grandmother, who occasionally provided her granddaughter with memorable treats. One such was on the occasion of the Silver Jubilee of King George V in 1935, when the Royal Yacht, the *Victoria and Albert*, laid anchor off Portsmouth, and Alice with her young charge were allowed on board. 'Grandma and some Petty Officers and I had radishes for tea! I remember telling my mother who couldn't believe I had had radishes on the royal yacht, and I sat on George V's bed with a sort of slippery golden eiderdown... good Lord, I've lived through several ages...'. The second memorial is invisible to the viewer, but appears in Rozanne's selection of materials. For example, the sailor's wreath is 'just bound in black, fine wool cloth cut on the bias so it wrapped easily and finished with a wide black ribbon bow, very old black ribbon I've had for a long long time – beautiful – that a lady had given to me who was mad about the Navy. She has been dead for about thirty years and wore a Union Jack vest, and said she wanted to be buried at sea. I've used pieces of material that Sybil, as she was called, gave me over the years as I have indeed used things that other people have given me. She would have been terribly thrilled to think this beautiful black, black ribbon looked like new on the wreath.' Intertwined throughout the work, then, are elements from Rozanne's collection of objects and materials that are private reminders of the giver, including – in *For Alice Hunter* – a tiny ball of Alice's tailor's wax saved and passed on to her by her Auntie Winnie.

RIGHT *Stretcher and body bag*, 2003. For burial at sea, tradition has it that the last stitch was through the deceased sailor's nose. Photograph by Philip Clarke, courtesy of the Mission Gallery.

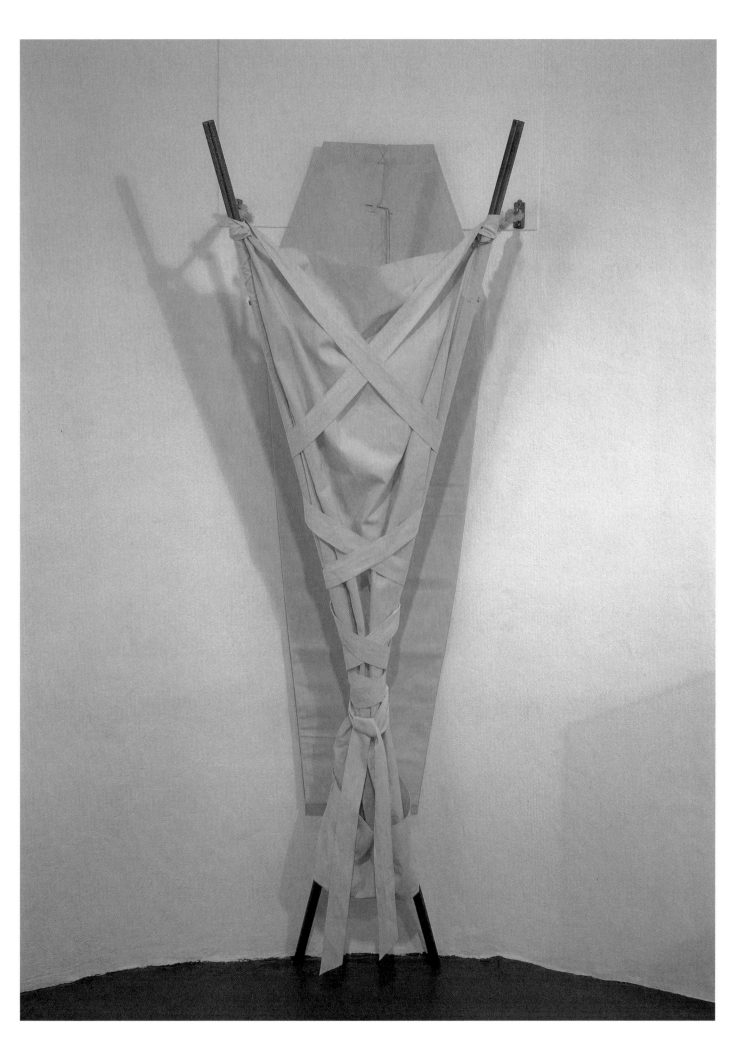

More important than the personal memorials is the way 'this work has grown from its origins... in an unafraid manner as a personal salute to Grandma without being sentimental [and] also became a salute... to people who served or died at sea over the last 120 to 150 years.' The latter began in earnest with the installation on *HMS Belfast*, where strips of calico, reminiscent of bandaging, were inscribed by Rozanne and tied to interior pipework. Visitors were invited to take a strip of material and write a memorial of their own. The result was a work entitled *In Memoriam*, which grew and grew as the exhibition – the first aboard the ship – attracted record numbers and had its run extended by ten weeks into February 2007. Messages were often simple but poignant, just one example being 'Dear Grandad, we never met but thank you for serving our country.' By the time of the Portsmouth showing, there were at least 400 strips, written on either side and set into gentle motion by a quiet fan. Of this mass of cream streamers, some short, some long, Rozanne herself found that it was 'extraordinary what they wrote, and it was their contribution you see; I was no longer part of it, it was Grandma or the seamstresses, the sailor and others' sailors, their memories. Pretty humbling really.'

The moving atmosphere that often surrounds her work may appear the result of a canny selection of subject matter, but there is nothing glib in Rozanne's choices. 'Whatever format emerges be it stark or ornate, my belief in... the detailing through research is of the greatest importance. Whether the discovered facts are thrown out or used, and whether hidden or used obviously or in allegorical mode, nevertheless they are vital...'.[3] In the case of *The Seamstress and the Sea*, much is hidden, and the final result has a starkness in part derived from the very limited use of colour: indigo denim and a vivid red pincushion in *For Alice Hunter*, or touches of red denoting wounds or surgeon's stitches. All else is cream and black, creating a subtle distinction between the seamstress and surgeon on the one hand, and naval personnel on the other, between those whose role was more peripheral but in the end, more readily delineated, and those thousands who served at sea, remaining anonymous yet appreciated nevertheless. The restrained colouration also belies the months of background research in its suggestion of simplicity, which in turn makes the core of the installation an emotional dialogue between objects and audience. This is entirely deliberate, for her intent is not to distract from the direct communication by her work to the viewer. 'I like work that one has to wait for – let it begin to speak.'

OPPOSITE *Memorial Wreath*, 2004, detail. The scarf draped around a bird's skull is a square of Macclesfield silk, known as a 'sailor's silk'.

LEFT *Memorial Wreath*, 2004. Photograph by Philip Clarke.

OVERLEAF *In Memoriam*, 2006–07, detail from the streamers inscribed by visitors to *The Seamstress and the Sea*. Photograph by Dil Bannerjee, courtesy of the Imperial War Museum.

My Great
Grandad was
cald Jack and
he served on
board. HMs
magic in world
war 2

Ayla

WHERE'S WILFRED?

Like so many of her generation, Rozanne found her childhood cut short by a radio broadcast on the 3rd of September, 1939, during which the Prime Minister, Neville Chamberlain, reluctantly announced that Britain was at war with Germany. It was the first time that such momentous news had been conveyed by radio to the populous. All, including Rozanne and her family, had been bracing for war for over two years, as Chamberlain had tried in vain to negotiate peace with Hitler. Thus with the German invasion of Poland on the first day of September, the British authorities were able to act immediately. Today on the internet evocative BBC broadcasts can still be heard, documenting the rapid movement of citizens: 'In the first four days of September 1939 nearly 3,000,000 people were evacuated from Britain's towns and cities and moved to safer places in the countryside. The vast majority of these were schoolchildren, but they were accompanied by 100,000 teachers and sometimes a parent.'[1] The evacuated children accounted for about 7.5 percent of the British population, and in that beautiful September – Rozanne remembers well the fine weather and how thoroughly her parents had prepared her for this 'adventure' – she and several other children were driven to Wiltshire by Miss Canning, one of her teachers. With Rozanne was her little gas mask and her pink and blue stuffed toy rabbit, named Wilfred.

The fate of her companion, Wilfred, is a tale that can no doubt be duplicated in essence by thousands of other children, but for Rozanne it accounts for her keen awareness of the talismanic qualities of inanimate objects. With most of her fellow evacuees installed in the Manor Farm in Oxenwood, two mothers and their children were given a nearby cottage. One of the women was very cold to the children. She was married to a major in the Royal Artillery, and Rozanne looked forward to moments when her husband came on leave, because he would read aloud to the children. Otherwise, it was Wilfred who kept her company, although he soon had no middle from being held so tightly. When Rozanne fell into a snowdrift, she became ill, but worse. Asking this same woman for Wilfred, she was told he was 'old and dirty', and he'd been burned. Homesickness overwhelmed her, she stopped eating, and became so sickened by food that she was ill at the table. Her father and mother came to visit, bringing a new Wilfred, white with gingham clothing, but this did nothing to calm her. She waved them off, holding back the sobs until they had departed, and was soon stammering when she spoke. The stammer lasted a long while and came and went over the years. Chuckling, she mischievously proposes that 'If someone were doing a great big tome about me in the Victorian times, they would say "she was a sickly child" and I've gone on being sickly since I fell in the snowdrift the first year of the War, never been right since really.' As a consequence of her fall, during the early months of 1940, she had developed rheumatic fever, pericarditis and attendant heart disease. Because German planes began dropping their bomb-loads on Wiltshire airbases in early June 1940, she was relocated to Wales, to Abercamlais, the ancestral home of a naval officer, Commander Garnons-Williams, and his WREN wife. Within two weeks Rozanne was in the hospital in Brecon, where they thought she was dying. A telegram summoned her parents, who took three days to travel by train from Portsmouth to Swansea, for the month was still June and the platforms were lined with soldiers returning from Dunkirk, among them Rozanne's mother's brother, Harry, who was in the Grenadier Guards.

The illness lingered, terminating Rozanne's stay in Wales and prompted her removal to Petersfield, only 18 miles inland from Portsmouth but deemed safe and, more importantly, providing the requisite drier climate. However, life was far from settled; her family home bombed and her father for a time living in a cellar, she recalls how he walked the streets seeking shelter for his family. In the end, she stayed at about eight different addresses, initially with her parents, then without her family, but soon in two rooms with her parents and new brother, who had been born in January 1941, during a three-day bombing raid on Portsmouth. They were joined by her grandmother, who continued sewing sailors' collars until her death in 1943 or '44. Just prior to eventually settling in Petersfield, the family shared half of a house that belonged to a naval surgeon, and Rozanne was fascinated by his books with diagrams of diseases. During this time Rozanne was not allowed to walk; once, being carried downstairs by her father in a guest house also home to two sailors, he prompted her to touch the passing sailor's collar secretly, 'so that he won't know', to bring luck to her and to the lad, enacting an old superstition to ward off drowning at sea.

Over the three years of her enforced confinement in bed, there was little to do but read and read and remember such moments, and the days that had gone before. Her mind would play over her months in Wiltshire, where in her little school every child but Rozanne had a parent in the Navy or Army, 'like Micky and Peter Martin,' she recounts, 'whose father was a Royal Marine and went down on *HMS Hood*.' Then there was Mrs Glover, whose husband was a major in the Royal Marines; her three children were Jimmy, Susan and Bill. The eldest boy, then 11, taught Rozanne and his siblings to play rugby; she recounts with some glee that during the rough and tumble of one game, 'he sat on my face and I bit his bottom – I remember his grey corduroy shorts…'. The same Jimmy became General Sir James Glover, a Commander in Chief of UK Land Forces from 1978 until 1987. Rozanne remembers his participation in a BBC1 *Panorama* broadcast, on 29 February, 1988, when he opened a path to the Irish peace talks by expressing his view that military defeat of the IRA was impossible and, in so doing, was acknowledged in June 2000, when he died, as having 'contributed significantly to [the] current political breakthrough north and south of the border.'[2] So despite the fact that her father remained at Lloyds Bank

in Portsmouth, which specialised in foreign exchange (so much so that he had scales given to him when he retired, and Rozanne retains a 'great brass doorstop, representing 200 Troy ounces,' to weigh money against the gold standard), her imagination became and remained saturated with military characters and consequences.

Although perfectly aware of the time-line of her own life, this pot-pourri of past events perfumes her present day environment, an analogy she acknowledges 'as long as the pot-pourri contains things that are sharp as well as pretty, not all rose petals, but laced with a dark spice.' Indeed, in looking over *Interesting War News,* a work of about 1980–81 (fired by a radio broadcast about the third battle of Ypres,[3] at Passchendaele, a battlefield eventually visited with her second husband Brian Hawksley), she reflects that 'war has haunted me.' This work was the first to incorporate bones.

Unlike other artists, whose work falls into stages or periods, each with distinguishing characteristics, Rozanne instead has adopted a range of aesthetics that appear as parallel lines of development, brought forward in her work as required by her creative intentions. As a result, the combination of a desiccated bird and other found materials also appears in use very recently in *Poppy Day,* also a response to war. The concept germinated while she listened to the radio on Armistice Day, the anniversary of the official end of World War I on 11 November 1918. On this occasion, in 2007, *The Observer* noted that 'serving soldiers horrifically injured in the Iraq and Afghan conflicts have been refused permission to join today's main Remembrance Day parade, prompting angry accusations that the Government is "ashamed" to have them seen in public.'[4]

LEFT *Interesting War News,* c.1980–81, giving the details of the losses involved in a gain of 25 yards. Photograph by Mike Sage.

ABOVE *Semana Santa: Death of Hope,* early 1990s. The entire is a purple velvet-lined box containing a crucified bird; it was a response to Rozanne's experience of Holy Week in Seville, in 1989.

OVERLEAF *Interesting War News,* detail.

Rozanne's retort was 'the same damn thing, yet once again...' and, in material form, the juxtaposition of a crucified bird and poppies, the latter the traditional symbol of remembrance of wars gone by. A bird's head alone, carrying a dried olive branch, adorns another board in *There is No Water...*, of the same period. It too is a reference to war, as well as to the destruction of the planet. It draws from 'What the Thunder Said', the fifth section of T.S. Eliot's poem, *The Waste Land*, written in 1922 and hailed by many for its portrayal of universal despair. In it also appears the line, 'Dry bones can harm no one.'[5] Finally, there is *Pax*, the most recent of the bird pieces, which incorporates a bayonet holder, the word 'Pax' torn from a missal, and found cloth poppies. In total, this group, with its twisted forms, broken lines, sumptuous colour and archaeological allusions are neo-mannerist in conception.[6]

LEFT *Poppy Day*, 2007, detail. Boxed-in to suggest imprisonment as well as the loneliness of socially isolated wounded soldiers.

TOP *There is No Water...*, c.2007, detail. The inscription, from T.S. Eliot's poem, *The Waste Land*, reads 'There is no water but only rock, Rock and no water, There is not even solitude in The Mountains.'

ABOVE *Pax*, 2008. Photograph by Philip Clarke.

The bones, while emblematic of differing specific moments or memories, are always suggestive of frailty to Rozanne. They form a backdrop, for example, to the figure of Christ on *Mitre for First Sunday in Lent* (1995) for which the inspiration was the moment '...then was Jesus taken up to be tempted.'[7] Thus in *Rozanne with Tabitha at Auntie Ada's 1933*, a self-portrait created during 2004 and 2005, a young fox's jawbone envelopes the image of two year-old Rozanne, who has included her year of birth on the left and, on the right, an empty space for the year of her death. Thus framed, the photograph of herself can be compared to another, taken with her mother, and encircled by a frame of plaited Woodbine cigarette packets. Ephemeral accessories such as this fill Rozanne's home and studio, providing a constant evocation of bygone pastimes, as well as a gentle reminder of the sunnier days of her childhood. For example, after her mother's sister, Winnie, had married, the summers during the 1930s had been spent in Radipole outside Weymouth, a time captured in *Radipole*. At Uncle Oogle and Auntie Winnie's was Flossie, their liver and white Springer, who 'talked to the parrot and lived in a beer barrel made habitable by Uncle, who looked after the horses for a local brewery.' By 1939 the couple had left their minute cottage to live in a council house on the outskirts of Weymouth, and it was here that Rozanne was taken to play with a bucket and spade on the coke mound at the local gas-works, to breathe in the fumes said to be good for her whooping cough, and here that they heard news of war.

TOP *Rozanne and Mother in Will's Wild Woodbine cigarette packet card mount*, c.1938.

ABOVE *Rozanne with Tabitha at Auntie Ada's 1933*, self-portrait, 2004–05.

RIGHT *Mitre for First Sunday in Lent*, 1995, detail. Painted bone, hand-stitching and jewels; the moiré silk, satin and lace were brought back from Spain in 1989. Now in the collection of Whitelands College, University of Surrey, Roehampton. Photograph by Brian Hawksley.

Flossie and Me, an assemblage made in 2007 for a temporary exhibition at the Imperial War Museum, collides memories of Flossie and Radipole in 1937–38 – when, if it was raining, they would go to The Needlewoman to buy embroidery transfers, the first of which for Rozanne was of a Red Setter – and of Rozanne's first awareness of her own uncertainties. She worried that upon evacuation she wouldn't be able to tie her own hair ribbon, and her mother advised her to lean against a wall to accomplish this task, hence the work's inclusion of a gas mask, be-ribboned.

Recovering from the rheumatic fever by 1943, Rozanne went to Petersfield High School, where 'I should say that I had no confidence at all. I could read, but I really didn't know the difference between adding up and taking away and I could only go in the mornings and the classroom was at the top and once up there I stayed put until I went home – because 'heart trouble' precluded going up and down stairs. My parents had very little money. Well, nobody did. But I really had, when I look back (and I've seen a photograph somewhere), a terrible hand-me-down that my mother put together out of other second-hand clothes and I had this straight hair. I must have looked eight, except I was so *huge*.

I mean bonily huge. I must have looked eight when I was about twelve.' Because Petersfield in those days was a market town, 'there were farmers' daughters there, all kinds of people, and then Battersea Girls' School came down and were evacuated near us, and so joining the Girl Guides I do remember being *terrified* of one girl from London, who literally said to me – and it sounds like a terrible cliché in a book – "hello Rozanne," she says, "my little skin and blister" and I was TERRIFIED because I thought it was something awful, that she didn't like me. But in fact, she did.' Looking back on this event, she stresses that 'what I'm *again* trying to say is that because I'd been locked up for about three years – locked up in bed, I should say – and because I was the age I was, I wasn't aware of the breakdown of social and class barriers.' And it was not really until 1948, when she went to art school, that she mixed with 'people who didn't speak as my father wished I would speak all the time. You know, distinctly and correctly, and not saying "ho" instead of "how". And if somebody asked me something, I was never to give what I thought was my real opinion but to say this, this, that and the other. So it was very difficult in a way, my first year at school...'.

LEFT Rozanne's collection of commemorative and souvenir china displayed on a dresser in her front room.

RIGHT *Flossie and Me*, 2007. Displayed in proximity to the Imperial War Museum's Children and War Gallery (a long term display).

Reinventing discarded objects, giving them a new artistic life, is a lynchpin of Rozanne's approach to materials. *Black Mirror* (2004) is also embellished with bones, as is its companion, *White Mirror*. The mirrors allude to Jean Cocteau's surrealistic film, *Orphée*, which was released in 1950 and includes the storyline that death comes and goes through a mirror. By this time Rozanne was an art student in Portsmouth, at the Southern College of Art (the other site being in Bournemouth). Rozanne attended for three years, receiving her NDD in 1951. There she met her first boyfriend, John, who had been in the Services and introduced her to the American Forces Network on the radio

– she recalls Vaughn Munroe's *Ghost Riders in the Sky* – and to jiving. She rode on the back of his motorcycle up to a hill above town, where they would sit looking at the lights below. They went together to the pictures three times a week, seeing America portrayed as a bright, perfect place. She was especially taken with the early space films and, holding John's hand, relished the moment when fictional characters got out of a space ship on to a new world. In this optimistic atmosphere, she accepted John's proposal of marriage, even though her father had reservations because 'John was a Methodist, looked like a handsome spiv, and had the slightest Hampshire accent.'

ABOVE *Black Mirror*, 2004.

TOP RIGHT *White Mirror*, 2004, detail. The use of mirrors refers to the notion that death comes and goes through a mirror, something reinforced by Rozanne's grandmother's habit of covering mirrors when a funeral cortege passed by, and also when it was going to thunder.

RIGHT *Libera me, domine, de morte aeterna*, glove, 1992, detail.

For her own part, Rozanne was disliked by John's father, because she had peroxided her hair and wore her own 'off-the-shoulder New Look frock, cork-soled canvas wedges and Outdoor Girl cyclamen lipstick.' Miss Gibbons at the art college concurred, describing the effect as 'so common', to which Rozanne cheekily replied, 'but it's been such a terribly hot summer, my hair got bleached at Weymouth.' The much later mirrors, embellished with jewels, lace, sequins and feathers, have an innocence as if filtered through the eyes and emotions of this young woman – a beauty derived from the tenderness with which each element is incorporated – and yet a sternness that rebukes the folly of vanity, and perhaps, of decisions quickly made and regretted. Certainly Rozanne regrets what she describes as her shabby treatment of her first beau, to whom she dutifully returned the engagement ring.

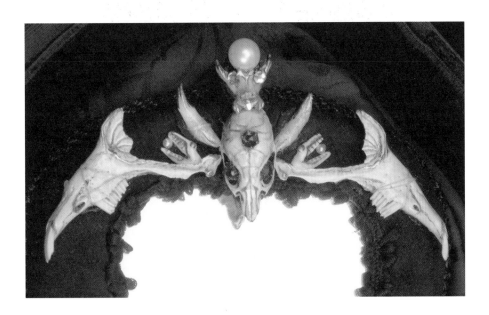

The fleeting nature of youth and beauty is a subject intertwined with Rozanne's assessment of her teenage years, and finds its representation in two works, the face mask *One has to be so careful these days* (2004) and a piece commissioned by Andrew Salmon for *10 x 10* (an exhibition at the 1999 Knitting & Stitching Show) entitled *I shall go The Way whence I shall Not Return*. The title of the latter comes from Job chapter XVI, verse 22, a passage often spoken at funeral services and one, it has been argued, that demonstrates the futility of a belief in resurrection.[8] Amid the complex symbolism employed on *A Mitre for the Bishop of London* (1997–98) is a human skull licked by flames, a further reference to 'our time on earth, our frailty.' Despite its richness, there is a sternness here too: 'I wished every mark to be of significance – no decoration for decoration's sake, no glitz, no glitter. ...On either side are the Star of David and the emblem of Islam,

reminders of East London and the Bishop's time as Bishop of Stepney, his affection for this multi-cultural area and its people together with his continuing interest in the world's philosophies and beliefs.'[9] That reference to broad-mindedness might also be said of Rozanne herself, whose wide-ranging philosophical perspectives appear to have begun with her three thoughtful years while ill. And just as her use of bones is representative of 'what is our armour and yet our fragility and breakability', her frequent allusions to death are not necessarily insinuations of morbidity, but rather 'a preoccupation which she accepts in a serene yet matter of fact way, because in her art she deals with images and symbolism which touch on the very fabric of life.' These comments, extracted from an edition of *The Western Mail* that also makes reference to her 'creative grit', adds her further comment on this apparent dichotomy: 'In fact, I'm a person who laughs a lot.'[10]

ABOVE *I shall go The Way whence I shall Not Return*, 1999. Commissioned by Andrew Salmon for *10 x 10*, an exhibition at the Knitting & Stitching Show of that year. In the collection of Andrew Salmon. Photograph by Rob Kennard.

RIGHT *One has to be so careful these days*, face-mask, 2004, detail. Exhibited at SOFA, Chicago, 2005.

ABOVE *A Mitre for the Bishop of London*, 1997–98.
The mitre was presented St James' Day, 25 July 1998,
when the Rt. Revd. and Rt. Hon. Richard Chartres was
made a Freeman of the Weaver's Company at the end
of his chaplaincy. Photograph by Bob Pullen.

RIGHT The lappets on *A Mitre for the Bishop of London*,
1997–98, detail. Showing the emblem of the Worshipful
Company of Weavers who commissioned the piece (left)
and a depiction of one of the Bishop's croziers, designed
by him (right). Photograph by Brian Hawksley.

OVERLEAF TOP LEFT *A Mitre for the Bishop of London*,
working drawing, 1996. Photograph by Brian Hawksley.

OVERLEAF BELOW LEFT *A Mitre for the Bishop of London*,
work in progress, 1996–97. Photograph by Brian Hawksley.

OVERLEAF RIGHT *A Mitre for the Bishop of London*,
1997–98, detail. Photograph by Bob Pullen.

It is essential, then, to add that there were many happy days in Portsmouth, among them hearing her Uncle Oogle play the saxophone and her Auntie Ada play the piano, which she had done professionally at the Victoria Cinema. Her son Rex, Rozanne's cousin, was also often there, and they would act out a story to Ada's musical accompaniment: 'I suppose he is about fifteen years older than I am. He was at Arnhem, 6ft 5ins tall, in the Lifeguards with Tommy Cooper, and when Tommy used to come down to the Theatre Royal at Portsmouth for a show, Rex, who had by then joined the Portsmouth police, used to go and have a drink with him – God we used to laugh such a lot...'. Ada, too, helped Alice, her mother-in-law, when the pile of sailors' collars grew too high, but aside from the constant exposure to stitching, many other influences from music, theatre and film were thus interlaced throughout these days. Her porous mind absorbed surrounding textures, colours and sounds in complete three-dimensionality, so that 'various encounters that have made their mark, reassessed when they appear as memories [are] important to me as I am now.' It is this that transforms materials from mere substances into objects cherished for their overlapping, nuanced meanings. 'I like wood, I like bone, I like jewels for what they are and what they do. I like fabric, I like thread – I like the dependency of one on the other, the often unseen intricacy. I like their connotations – their association with man, their capabilities. My background, which at one time I rejected, is bound up with these qualities...'.

MAN ABOUT TOWN

The year is 1951. 'Then I heard I'd got in and I shut myself in the lavatory in Portsmouth *practically* for the whole day. I remember various members of staff coming and saying "Oh you must go, go for me, go for me." "NO, I don't wanna go..." At *last*, somebody said, "well, you can change departments when you get there." Well, I couldn't. When I did get there I tried to but I couldn't.' Rozanne had obtained one of only eight places offered that year to study fashion at the Royal College of Art (RCA) in London – in a department formed in 1948 and then the only postgraduate study available in the UK for this subject. The ups and downs of her time at the Royal are vividly captured in her own words, which also illuminate the world of London art students during the early 1950s. Her trajectory thereafter, and until the mid-1960s, placed her increasingly in what would then have been called a man's world, as she struggled to become both independent and a bread-winner, all the while dodging the pitfalls of impetuous, youthful decisions.

What becomes clear in listening to Rozanne's stories about the Royal College is her capacity to evoke a mood or scene, to bring a three-dimensionality to life. However skillful in speech, this talent is even more evident in material form, as is apparent in *From a Jack to a King – Greed*, a work of 1998. Indeed, she had always wanted to sculpt – having been introduced to it at the art college in Portsmouth – and it was also in her blood. Her great uncle Charles James Pibworth (1878–1958) had been a sculptor. She never knew him, but had been told he did portraits and busts, as well as architectural relief carvings and a bird bath, standing in gardens near London's Albert Bridge and commemorating the founding of the Women's Police Service in 1915. When she departed for London, her father told her 'Uncle Charles is still alive – his studio is in King's Road – do go.' But she wouldn't. 'So foul...,' she says of her youthful defiance, but it is telling that what she does relate with some pride is the fact that work was given to Eric Gill because Pibworth wouldn't compromise. A familial parallel can be found here too, in Rozanne's own convictions. And, as we shall see, her determination to set her own course might also be said to be a genetic inheritance from her father's side, in this case from Samuel Smiles, a Victorian philosopher whose publication, *Self Help*, became an immediate bestseller when issued in 1859; its avocation of the allied virtues of hard work, thrift, and perseverance has been described as the precursor of current motivational and self-help literature, and it is still in print today.[1]

Rozanne's own account of her days at the Royal College give ample evidence of her belief in the right of social advancement. Of her growing awareness of the breakdown of class barriers she remembers 'saying to my mother (it sounds so dreadful) when I went home on holiday, "There's this great guy, he's the most *wonderful* illustrator and his dad's a window cleaner." Well, my mother was delighted, 'cause that was what *she'd* come from really. My father I think nearly fainted, because he probably thought everyone else who got into the Royal College was going to be terribly well off and well connected.

That's another reason I think I hated the Fashion School, because of the *pretentiousness* that went on, and you know it was "darlings this" and "darlings that" and very very affected. That's the way it was. That's the way one had to be. That affectedness, which I found so shallow, was shown up by the majority of the rest of the college and what I was learning about life.' In a similar vein, she recalls someone 'in the graphic school, painting... poor background, like a lot of us, just always wore the same thing day after day. I went up in the music room one day and there was this bloke, who I expect my father would've not let me speak to as a child – (*why* he should be like that, I don't know, my dad, I mean). So there was this bloke at the piano and I was knocked out. I just sat and listened and he said, "hello", he said, and I said "isn't that *tremendous*. What is it? I didn't even know you could play." "Oh yes," he said, "I love music, and this is Bartok." *Well*. Me, who'd been told by my father that Elgar, Handel and Parry were *the* composers. You see, that's been with me all these years, that kind of memory.'

The vividness with which such recollections are engraved in Rozanne's mind emphasise her 'in the round' perception of people and places. Her musical ear plays its part in this process, not least because music seemed to set her free from the constraints of the Fashion School.

It was not only a straightforward means of enjoyment, although it was most certainly that too; she recollects with relish a famous pianist known for his Mozart, Denis Matthews: '...he used to come to the music room, which was at the top of the Common Room building, and just play and play for hours. And Segovia! He was in London to perform – but *he* came and gave us an impromptu recital, just like that! The Common Room was quite extraordinary, the people that wandered in and out; it was a hub for all the arts.' Music was also part of a wider social network that began with the Royal College but quickly extended outwards to clubs such as the Gargoyle. At the Colony Room Club – opened in 1948 and now famous for 'the fact that Bacon, arguably the most significant painter of the post–war era, made Belcher's club his second home'[2] – Ted Dicks took over Mike McKenzie's spot at the piano one summer, and it was Ted and a couple of other chaps with whom Rozanne shared Len Deighton's basement in her final year at the Royal. Ted himself was described in 1954 as 'a solid man on any combo this side of Muswell Hill [and] wields a cool brush in the college painting department where he is negotiating his third hectic year. A leading rowdy in RCA social life, when he gets together with Bruce Lacey all hell breaks loose.'[3]

ABOVE Collage of RCA memorabilia, including a photograph of Ted Dicks by Adrian Flowers, from *ARK 10*, the 1954 edition (edited by Len Deighton) of the College magazine.

RIGHT Two fashion sketches created while a student at the Royal College of Art, London, 1951–54.

'First year was the basics of design: flat cutting, sizing, fitting, things like that. One of the first things said to us was, "right, everyone to do a stitched and bound button hole." I couldn't. I was so kak-handed, so I did a huge one (bound I think) and said, "well I'd only have one button on the coat anyway." Of course, we were expected to be able to cut to a reasonable level. I didn't know what cutting on the stand and toile-making was. Mrs Garland would go to see the Paris collections and buy toiles from a couture house. That's to say, an exact copy, made in calico, of the particular style that she liked. Of that style, she'd bring back three or four. They cost the earth. And they would be passed round. We had to cut a pattern exactly, without taking the dress apart. It's quite easy, actually, once you know how to look for the grain directions and other clues. Second year, I did tailoring and a specialism. Mine was millinery, which I loved. There was a French woman, one of two visiting milliners; the one for the third years was Monsieur somethingorother... French, who was, we thought, having an affair with a third year, if you can call that kind of thing an affair. We had a lot of outside people, which was extremely good – actually all of the teaching staff worked elsewhere in trade or couture. There was Mrs Fields Rhodes, who

would come in once a week. She was a very kind and knowledgeable woman as well as being fabulous at fitting. Can't remember who she worked for. And there was Mr Lipman, who taught tailoring and its cutting, and he was fabulous. I mean, I hardly dared go in the room, I felt so ashamed.'

'At that time in London there were a number of couturiers. There was Lachasse, Norman Hartnell, Hardy Amies, Charles Creed, Digby Morton, oh a lot. And we were sent to see their collections. Their showroom/ workrooms were usually in rather nice houses in the Piccadilly-Park Lane area around Mayfair, fitted with grey carpets and the little gold chairs always borrowed from Harrods. There was one whose work I liked very much, John Cavanagh. Very simple, beautifully cut, fitted and made. (Rare, I have to say.) Madge Garland said one morning, "Rozanne, David (David Watts, who became head designer at Jaeger later), you will go to Norman Hartnell's tomorrow morning and you will report back to me and I wish to see your drawings plus notes." Well, of course, we're not allowed to draw there, so you had to sit with eyes peeled and draw – not in a coffee or wine bar, there weren't any – but it was terribly useful, we used to go to the Dorchester to go to the loo, have a cup of tea and draw. Going to the loo in the

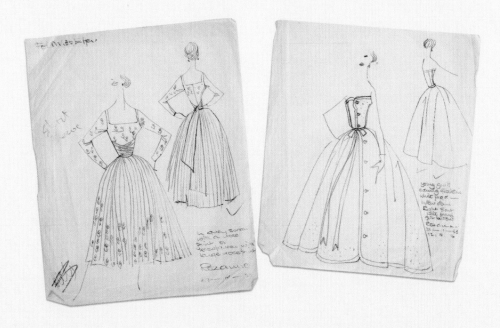

Dorchester, God! But it was good, going and seeing how all the clothes were constructed. They were often dull, somehow. The materials were fabulous, but there was only Cavanagh and sometimes Hardy Amies and sometimes Charles Creed. He could be good. We'd go to them all, twice a year. But they were not a patch on Paris. (Later I went to its couture houses with my own students.)'

'Hartnell's. Well, this particular show... there was one model called Delores, who was rather beautiful – black hair pulled back in a bun chignon – and we thought that the making was not at all good. Delores swirled round in one of the ball dresses... the bodice was nicely fitted, but something was very wrong with the skirt, and it looked like bar tacks holding it together. And as she swept past us – we were sitting with our backs to the window, luckily – she'd say, "oh, lovely work, lovely work..." and David, who was a terrible giggler when he wasn't being sarcastic, just started. And I started. And we couldn't stop. It was appalling. Luckily, it was towards the end. It was very very rude of us. But at the end I clapped my white gloves together and David picked up his furled umbrella and we trotted out and we just fell about with laughter the whole of the way down the street at this awfulness. The next morning we were both summoned into Madge Garland's office. "I hear that you were thrown out of Hartnell's." And we said, "well, no, we weren't thrown out, Mrs Garland, but we left pretty quickly" and we really got – quite rightly, quite rightly, because we were guests – got absolutely shrunk to about half an inch by her tongue. And David, being a very very very good tailoring student, didn't have so much to worry about, but I did, because, you know, I could hardly say "well, my work's better than theirs." Mind you, I think it was, from certain points of view!'

'Madge Garland, who would now be called Professor Garland, had been Editor of American Vogue. Extremely chic. She would come into the Fashion School about three or four times a week... unexpectedly. She looked like Edith Evans, I always thought. Indeed, when I saw Edith Evans in The Chalk Garden, I was so terrified that it was Madge, I almost had to leave! Anyway, Madge would come in a Jacques Fath suit.

Beautifully cut of course, usually a sort-of grey lavender-y, that kind of colour, and a little veiled hat and shoes by Ferragamo. And when we heard the taxi door slamming outside 21 Ennismore Gardens, where the Fashion School was, some of us would faint with fear and others would smile smugly. A lovely student, Kenneth Burgess – who went to Marks & Spencer afterwards and absolutely lifted the place up (I mean Marks & Spencer's design) – once had hysterics and really wept, and I certainly was terrified. Once I was called in: "Rozanne, will you please go into Mrs Garland's office...". "Yes..."; so I went in and waited. And there was Madge, back to the window as ever, beautiful little violet velvet hat, beautifully groomed, and I stood there. It seemed like half an hour until she put her pen down and looked up. You know, like an editor in a movie. She said, "Rozanne, I wish to talk to you." "Yes, Mrs Garland." Eventually she continued, "I have been told that you have been seen in the Fulham Road in trousers. Is that so?" "Yes Mrs Garland." There was a terrible silence and I think I must have gone unconscious after that for a bit. She next said, "Never, never, never, let it be said that one of my girls was seen in trousers. You may go." (Back to prison and the chains and bread and water...) Now this is because two of us had gone to Millets in Leicester Square where we knew that a consignment of Black Watch regimental trews were coming in; we each bought a pair, shortening and tailoring them more. And that's what I had on. But you see, in the early 1950s the fashion consisted of tightly belted pencil-slim skirts or a full circular skirt worn with white gloves, kitten heeled shoes and over a back-to-front cardigan, usually black, a little white collar. I got mine from Woolworths: men's paper collars, 1/6d for six. So about being seen in trousers. This really was the story of my life at the Fashion School. I was so unhappy and felt inadequate and unintelligent. I knew I'd gone into the wrong school and I got into all kinds of trouble, some quite trite. Like with Bernard Neville, for example, who was only with us in my second year. He and I were caught on the cutting room table playing the balcony scene from Noel Coward's Private Lives.'

'I'm going to whiz back and mention my first year again. A senior student, a lovely bloke called Peter Rice (who was married to Patty Albeck, equally lovely textile design student) was studying theatre off his own bat. He picked me to play Eurydice in Jean Cocteau's *Orphée*, for which he designed an amazing set. I thought that was terrific, you know, I was so pleased. The other play in the double bill was *The life and death of Tom Thumb the Great* by Fielding and I was cast as Princess Huncamunca in it, a rather sex-mad, yet innocent fetching sort-of person. The sets for the latter were done by Bernard Myers and a man called Lewin Bassingthwaite and yes, we've seen it all more recently, but then they were terrific. The sets were like black and white engravings, the costumes penny-plain and tuppence-coloured. You know, and all the declamation of gesture that went with that style. It was a romp, a pastiche. *Orphée* on the other hand was serious stuff. I was dead nervous, but that's the only part of my time I think I enjoyed in the first year. Anyway, at the end of the performance two people jumped up onto the stage with a huge bouquet, saying "come over for drinkies afterwards darling" and it was Johnny Minton and Francis Bacon, and that was the start of – I'm not going to say a "great" friendship – but rather a nice one. Johnny Minton was a complex man, a brave man indeed, hating his homosexuality, but he could be frighteningly entertaining. Always kind to his students. I also remember David Sylvester, the art critic and biographer who wrote the most accurate books on Francis Bacon. A large dark-haired man, shy, I think, and gentle. I remember being in his rooms in South Kensington once with a friend of mine, Ted Dicks – you know these tall grey rooms with one bulb hanging down – and David stood and sort-of swayed backwards and forwards for about two hours, reading his book on Rodin. Just round the corner from the Common Room building in Cromwell Road was a flat up two flights of stairs that was Francis Bacon's studio and I went there several times. Talk about seeing dedication! It made me realise – I think in retrospect even more – how wonderful it is (if I can couple my mind with Francis Bacon's) to be utterly involved with what you are doing in the way that he obviously was. Everything he did was wholehearted – working, drinking, laughing, talking abrasively or gently, and he was always courteous to me. His studio, not large, was full of paint, paper, canvas and cuttings everywhere.

LEFT Rozanne and Brian Aldridge in *Tom Thumb*, an RCA theatre production of 1952. Photograph by Clifford Hatts, courtesy of Special Collections, The RCA Library.

ABOVE Rozanne as 'Principal Boy' in a pantomime at Manresa House, c.1970. Photograph by Bert Isaac.

ᴀʙᴏᴠᴇ Rozanne as Lucy Lockett in *The Beggar's Opera*,
performed in the RCA Common Room Theatre in
March 1953, with all the costumes designed by her.
Photograph by Clifford Hatts, courtesy of Special
Collections, The RCA Library.

That first sight, I think – well, I know – underlined the fact that I was in the wrong school. I really was. But it made me soak up all I could in the other departments, with the painters, in seminars and so on.'

'In the next year came a production of *The Beggar's Opera* by John Gay. Again directed by Myers, this was 1953, the time the Olivier film came out and, actually, *The Times* said, if you want to see a real, bawdy, lusty version, go to the Royal College of Art, where *The Beggar's Opera* is on. I played Lucy Locket, the daughter of the jailer who gets pregnant by MacHeath. I designed the costumes and set up the workroom in the Common Room building. There were hardly any printed materials, and certainly none that would be right so I took the motif of stripes imitating the prison bars, as the whole of the opera took place within Newgate Jail. David Gentleman had designed a black, grey and white set; the colours were the costumes... a lot of it was taking basic colours of fabric, plain, whatever we could get our hands on and machining ribbons and tapes on to them, so they almost looked like drawings. Of the lace, I said, "no real lace at all, it's all got to be painted," so it was, onto calico. The only ready-made pieces were wigs and boots from Bermans. Anyway, it looked quite good, really.'

'The art colleges that we had the most social links with were Camberwell, the Slade and St Martins. Now Joe Tilson was at the latter before he came on to the RCA painting school. John Bratby, I remember, churned out work all the time... it's this dedication to work again. I should say that Robin Darwin was Head of the College at that time, and in the Painting School there was Robert Buhler, Ruskin Spear, Rodrigo Moynihan and John Minton as well as visiting painters. Among the students I remember Ed Middleditch and Jack Smith, who along with Bratby had to be labelled – but not at the time they were doing them – as the "kitchen sink school". It wasn't affectation. Most of them were living in pretty crappy conditions, you know, and had babies, or a baby perhaps, with things littered about in a kitchen that was a living room like we all did. So that was a kind of natural thing. They painted what they saw

and knew. When you think, you'd go to a "hop" at, say, College or St Martins, and you'd be drinking – certainly not wine – but half a pint of bitter or mild, whatever it was called and that was it. You saw a few people being violently ill, but they had probably only drunk about two pints altogether the whole evening. We did not have the money. The Common Room did a damn good lunch and we could have a poached egg on toast or a little salad or something in the evening if we could afford it. We also walked everywhere and at any time of night, for miles. No wonder we were all very thin.'

'At one point I lived in Battersea in a terrible room and a girl who was going to share with me refused to because it was "south of the river" and "had lino, my dear", so I paid for it by myself for a bit. I had various vacation jobs... to keep one's terrible room on. (You know, one room with a gas ring and, with luck, a fire that needed a penny in the meter every few minutes.) One job was serving on the fabric department at Derry & Toms in Kensington High Street around the time of the last big fog that crept into the houses. Another was in Jay's in Oxford Circus... a nice department store originally famous as the mourning emporium. I worked in the inexpensive millinery, which was on the ground floor in a howling draught; handbags on the left; better class millinery upstairs. There was a jolly little girl and me serving. Now – apart from a beret – we had two shapes of hats. There was your stitched felt, like a brimmed basin, of terrible quality felt with machine stitching round and round. The other one was like a bicycle clip really, that fitted over your head, with some feathers and ruched velvet. If someone asked for a larger size felt, there probably weren't any. You'd say "Yes, if you'd like to take a seat, madam" and with the hat go out the swing doors by the lift where it was just like walking into a black fridge, it was so cold, and bung it on a hat block in the stock room, turning the handle until the stitches nearly cracked, and then you'd bring it back and say, "Would this one fit you better madam?" If they wanted smaller ones, you had to ask them to wait till the smaller sizes came in. The little hats – bicycle clips – were

worn so often (look at photos of young women in the 1950s and still up to the '60s with these things clamped on their heads). These could bite into your head and they could spring off. I know, because I remember serving a customer and the other girl was over serving another one and we'd had to dress the department that morning and we'd put several of these bicycle clip hats on to the type of mannequin head that looks over its shoulder with the scarf tastefully draped around it, and as we were both serving, there was a noise and something like a bird shot between us and it was one of the hats. The bicycle clip – the alice band, to be honest – had worked its way up the head and shot with force across the department. How we kept a straight face I don't know. I mean it's not funny now, but in that very genteel situation, well...'.

'In my third year I also specialised one day a week in children's clothes. We were taught by a lovely lady, Mrs Gordon; she and her husband had set up a successful children's wear trade firm – rare then. We had to cut and calculate to the spare quarter of an inch. We learnt the whole process including finishing, folding, boxing and presentation. Just learnt the whole thing. The Fashion School held a show at the end of each year, and for this the top models were contracted and we were able to do one

or, at the most, two fittings. My children's clothes were modelled by Virginia, the daughter of Janey Ironside, Mrs Garland's assistant (who in 1956 replaced her). I think Mrs Garland – or Lady Ashton as she became – saw some hope in me as I whizzed through children's clothes, 'cause there wasn't much hope for making a living with the milliners!... Anyway, would I go to Marks & Spencer – I think it was Mr Schnieder who was there then, who wore purple eye shadow – and set up the children's wear department, and I said "No", "I wouldn't, I wouldn't", "I can't." Well, to get your DesRCA as we were in the Design School... you had to do a year in industry. And I said I wouldn't. There was talk between Madge Garland and Robin Darwin, and Madge said, "well, she won't go to industry, what are we going to do?" (I was told this afterwards. We were all quivering outside, wondering whether we'd got our degrees or not.) Anyway, Robin Darwin apparently said, "you know, seeing her progress through the College, and all those costumes we must give her a fine art degree." So I had an Associateship to the Royal College of Art, like the painters and sculptors. I didn't have to go into industry. And looking back, I'm quite proud that I wrote a degree thesis entitled *The Evolution of the New Woman*.'

An unmentioned rowdy was Rozanne herself, who adds, 'For a brief time in my last year there was a very exclusive club called the Dodo Club. There was Bruce Lacey, who invented 'performance art' before it was called performance art, and Ted Dicks, Len Deighton and Johnny Dankworth and Cleo Laine, Spike Milligan and his wife (I remember when they first joined: she, poor soul, heavily pregnant). We met down by Chelsea Reach and somebody – it was probably Bruce Lacey actually – made a wonderful dodo. But that folded within a year and we all went our various ways...'.

In Rozanne's case, she went straight off to *MAN and his Clothes*, where she took over as the 'Man to Man' columnist, her first efforts appearing in the November 1954 edition. In it, her sense of fun is immediately apparent, for example under the sub-heading, 'All Clear' in which she noted that: 'The Bristol Tattoo Club we hear mark invitations to their dinners: "Shirts will *not* be worn." This need not however cause undue alarm and despondency, as we assume they generally arrive wearing something. In any case it is obvious that these chesty affairs provide an opportunity for the progressive shirt designer. It can only be a matter of

time before a transparent shirt appears on the market. Manufactured in plastic material it would give an uninterrupted view of the wearer's torso plus any extraneous embellishments.'[4] At first glance an unlikely position, perhaps, it was offered to her precisely because she ran with the 'men about town'. The job offer was made, in fact, at the Studio Club, '*the* "in place" in Swallow Street, Piccadilly, for writers, artists, advertising people, musicians... a lot of US musicians were coming over and after performing late-night jazz at the BBC, extemporised at the Studio Club.' (Exhibitions were also held here, most notably those of 1953 and 1954 that established the Picassoettes – William Newland, Margaret Hine and Nicholas Vergette.) Rozanne worked for the magazine's editorial director, Tom Cundall, and alongside Jack Higgins, Editor of *Music Mirror*, a companion magazine also published by Century Press, which operated from a ramshackle house off Oxford Street, with its presses in the basement.[5] As well as her own column, she recalls 'spending hours 'til about 9 o'clock at night, trying to draw a portrait of Stravinski ready to go to press in the morning,' adding, 'I used to hear a lot of the tittle-tattle going on'.

LEFT Examples of Rozanne's illustrations for *Pattern Cutting for Beginners*, co-produced with Pamela Lee and published by Granada Publishing Ltd., London, in 1984.

ABOVE & OVERLEAF Examples of illustrations to her column, 'Man about Town' in *MAN and his Clothes*, these appeared in the January, March and July issues of 1955. Images courtesy of The British Library.

On occasion, she accompanied one of the main photographers ('who always wore an old trilby hat – tilted to one side – and sort of fancied himself somewhat, 'cause there weren't many photographers around, really, unless they were in Fleet Street'). One day she found herself with this photographer at a hotel in Park Lane, at a reception for Doris Day: '...and I remember being so embarrassed by this cake that had been made for her... This terrible oblong cake that was supposed to look like a Grundig tape recorder! Well it was just awful. I mean it was melty chocolate with white and silver on it. It could have looked beautiful and kitschy, but... it was all somehow terribly dull and in dubious "good taste". They probably thought that was absolutely amazing but it didn't go far enough...'. 'Anyway, somebody said "Miss Day will be coming downstairs any minute" and I have to say I saw, apart from the couturiers work I'd seen in Paris, this most beautifully cut and tailored black suit that Doris Day had on... it made her look very slim and elegant, and *tall*. I noticed this nipped-in waist on the suit jacket, with a slightly full basque, longish slim skirt, *beautiful* black shoes, black gloves, a choker of pearls I think, probably a diamond here or there – very discreet – hair dressed back plainly and beautiful

little pillbox hat. I *think* there was a little eye veil as well. She looked very elegant and was terribly nice. But god knows what she thought of the cake!' Despite Rozanne's desire to avoid working in the fashion industry, her appreciation of three-dimensional perfection obliterated any awe of Doris Day.

Equally revealing is her meeting with Billy Eckstine. '...wonderful black singer from the States, with his own recording company, with quite a vibrato to his warm, deep voice. On some occasion, taken along to a reception, there was this tall very attractive personality and he'd come to sign a contract as well. I'm not quite sure what I was doing there! We had a lovely cold lunch, and I talked to him a lot. Can't remember what we talked about – obviously music – but I <u>do</u> remember fingering his coat, which he wore all the time (probably frozen) and saying what fabulous fabric it was. And he said, in a deep voice, something like "Honey, this is vicuña mixed with cashmere." *Well!* I'd never heard of vicuña. I didn't know what one was! It was the most beautiful fabric I have ever felt in my life.' Her descriptions also tell of a character determined to communicate the nuances of every situation; she remembers what people say by remembering the sound of their voices, and her haptic perceptions are especially profound.

She is perfectly aware of the potential irony of her love of cloth and toile making – a three-dimensional activity – as opposed to flat work: 'It's odd isn't it? Although I was so put off and so terrified because both at art college and the Royal I could not make sense of flat cutting – it seemed so cold, so remote – nevertheless I held memories of the *feel* of beautiful fabric, what fabric does and how you can use it on the bias or on the straight. And you don't <u>make</u> it do things actually, you work <u>with</u> it. You can pad it out; you can shrink it and stretch it, do the most wonderful things with it.' Of this time of Dior's New Look, when jackets and dresses were cut to fit, she continues, 'They were cut so you could *move* in them, but it wasn't the outer fabric that fitted tightly or was strained, it was the underlying canvassing, bridals and stay tapes, and the holding stitches. That inner structure fitted absolutely in the best work and the outer fabric seemed to sculpt the body with no effort or visible means. Fabulous.'

Having taught there one day a week for a year, in September 1955 Rozanne began teaching at Guildford two then three days each week, leaving her position at *MAN and his Clothes* as a result. She loved the teaching, loved the students: 'When I first started, at my behest on London visits we would walk down Savile Row and look down into the basements with their enlarged windows, to see the tailors sitting cross-legged on tables or wide sills – it being easier to stitch across the knee – and with a little knowledge recognise the different kinds of canvas, shears and various tailoring irons, which are very heavy. As work progresses, the combined wool and canvas pieces are put over an appropriately shaped "ham" to shrink or stretch as need be. The steam is pressed into the piece first with damp cloths and then banged into it with a padded block or roll. When Terylene was first invented we were taken along to a mill making this polyester fabric. The factory had experimented on a man's jacket, and a strapless dress for a woman, and of course... the man's jacket looked appalling because you couldn't shrink Terylene and they must have treated it in the traditional way of shrinking and stretching, and of course it didn't work.'

Although no longer at the magazine, her jazzy social life continued. And it was at the Studio Club that Rozanne found her next accommodation, through Pat Braithwaite, the recently divorced ex-wife of Humphrey Lyttleton, the trumpeter and bandleader who influenced the British jazz scene for more than half a century and became the chairman of BBC Radio 4's *I'm Sorry I Haven't a Clue*.

The flat – a bed sitting room with a sink and gas stove at the back and still containing Humph's harmonium – was in Walpole Street, in Chelsea, where Àsgeir Scott, a noted illustrator eleven years her senior, lived on the floor above. Scott woo'd her with his intelligence, and his beautiful voice and manner. He did not have any interest in the theatre, still very much alive in Rozanne. For example, the night after its English-language premiere at the Arts Theatre, on 3 August 1955, she had gone with some of her students from Guildford to see Beckett's *Waiting for Godot*, directed by the 24-year-old Peter Hall; opening to hostility, within a week it was the rage of London. Not surprisingly, she also relished the performances of the English

Stage Company, ensconced under George Devine and Tony Richardson at the Royal Court from April 1956. There, through one of Scott's drinking crowd, a reader at J. Arthur Rank, she saw the 1958 premiere of Joan Plowright and Roy Dotrice in *The Chairs* and *The Lesson*, both by Eugene Ionesco. However, she and Àsgeir did have in common the experience of illness. He, a conscientious objector, had through his father – a director of Unilever, which had a whaling fleet – instead gone to sea as a flenser. On the *M/T South Africa*, torpedoed in 1942 in the Antarctic, his subsequent ten-day lifeboat journey led to tuberculosis and recuperation in a sanatorium, where fellow patients included the writer, Paul Jennings and

the most highly decorated RAF officer of World War II, Leonard Cheshire, with whom Rozanne remained in contact on occasion for a further fifty years.[6]

Rozanne and Àsgeir were married in Chelsea Old Church in June 1956 and thereafter, for some two decades, there is little else to document her life, artistic or otherwise. The years passed as years do when there is nothing but rushing from one responsibility to another. Within six months of the birth of Mathew in September 1957, she was up at dawn to a baby-minder in Chelsea with Mathew and on the 7:30am train from Victoria to Brighton Art College to teach two days a week, hastening back to the baby-minder and home, now in Royal Avenue, Chelsea. Soon after Mathew turned two the Scotts moved to Cornwall, so distant from friends and family, and making the teaching impossible. Nevertheless, while residing in Wesley Square, Mousehole, they remained close to Adrian Ryan, Scott's closest friend since their shared days at the Slade in 1939–40, and to Michael and Madeline Canney, whose gallery in Newlyn helped the St Ives school along.[7] Money lent by a friend fond of Mathew allowed the purchase of a fishing cottage in Newlyn's Boase Street, but soon many Newlyn and St Ives contacts were severed as a result of a row between Francis Bacon and Scott. He would travel alone to London to gather in and deliver commissions for illustrations, but drink most of his earnings away. (Although Bacon is said to have led the pack in the legendary combination of art and alcohol at the Colony, a private 'den',

Scott was often there too. He was also often in Chelsea and Fulham Road pubs and clubs, together with Lucien Freud, Laurie Lee – an usher at the Scott wedding – Lord Kilbracken, Stephen Spender, Cyril Connolly, James Cameron and the rest of the 'intellectual art set'.)

Meanwhile, Rozanne herself had revived her work for the Women's Home Industries (WHI), with which she had become involved, in their London knitwear showroom in 1956, as a result of Àsgeir's friendship with Beatrice and Dario Bellini. As she sat on the quay and painted canvases for the WHI, surviving on an erratic dressmaking business specialising in odd-sized women, together with borrowed coal and fish left at the door by local fisherman, she was forced slowly and unwillingly into a two-dimensional role so antithetical to the three-dimensionality that was naturally hers.

LEFT Collage of memorabilia relating to Rozanne's marriage to Àsgeir Scott, including three examples of his work and a photograph of him for a Kellogg's advertisement, taken by Bert Hardy for J. Walter Thompson.

ABOVE Rozanne and Mathew in Cornwall, early 1960. One thinks of Fred Astaire's line, spoken by a character based on Richard Avedon (photographer for *Harpers* 1945–65) in the 1957 film, *Funny Face*, who asked, 'What's wrong with bringing out a girl who has character, spirit, and intelligence?'

Audrey Levy, who visited during this period, could hardly believe that the Rozanne Scott she found – 'a cowed skeleton' – was the same person as the sparky Rozanne Pibworth she'd known at the Royal College. Looking back at it now, Rozanne sees that she vanished, absorbed as she was in her life with a man whose intelligence she admired, but whose drinking and brutal dismissal of her worth was no match for her. It was a cruel, crushing experience, brought to a close within a year of the birth of Joanna, who only survived for ten days in May 1961. Her escape to her parents, engineered by removing her belongings a suitcase at a time into a railway station locker, was prompted

finally when Mathew became the brunt of Àsgeir's temper.

These years were defining in terms of her sense of self and milieu, yet her surviving few works of this period have a kind of ominous anonymity, as she herself increasingly came to occupy a social space akin to wallpaper. Although his own fashion illustrations for *The Observer* were often based on Rozanne's quick sketches, Scott was derisory of her work for the WHI.[8] This limited company had been initiated in 1947 by Stella, Lady Reading (1894–1971), who had also founded what today is the Womens' Royal Voluntary Services. The role of the WHI was to capitalise on Lady

Reading's experience in Anglo-American cooperation, by providing work for British women – primarily through knitting and needlework, or 'tapestry' – that earned dollars for the UK. It's first success was the Manhattan auction, at $10,000, of six tapestry chair seats described as '[stitched] by Queen Mary and donated...'.[9] Beatrice Bellini had been delegated the improvement of standards, and with the knitting side already producing high quality goods (Eleanor Roosevelt in 1951 had declared that she had 'never before seen such wonderfully knitted things'),[10] attention turned to the needlework component. At the American end was Lady Harlech, first wife of the British Ambassador to the Kennedy administration and through her and Lady Reading, it seems, Mrs G. Howland Chase came into the Pimlico WHI shop seeking someone to head up her American Needlework Center in Washington DC. Rozanne, now teaching at Brighton and Portsmouth as well as designing and working WHI tapestries, was offered the position, which included an apartment above the Center on 20th Street NW and schooling for Mathew in Virginia.

Having to delay her arrival until January 1964 due to the assassination of President Kennedy, Rozanne never really settled, nor did Mathew, and by 1967 they were both back in the UK, where she returned to the WHI, painting designs and living above the shop, which she managed. But Mrs Chase had been extremely kind, treating Rozanne as a daughter and providing the setting in which Rozanne taught crewel work, *gros point* and

petit point to clients such as Lady Harlech and Mrs Robert Kennedy, and designed a rug for the Kennedy Center (having already designed one, in England, for Eleanor Roosevelt). Her work, including lecturing and teaching out of town, contributed to the recent assessment of the American Needlework Center as, in its prime, a prestigious institution: 'the oldest and most renowned needlework shop in the [area].'[11] Both before and after her few years in America, she had also boosted the status of the WHI tapestry side, taking commissions, often, from Daphne, Lady Straight, whose husband's mother was Dorothy Elmhirst, co-founder of Dartington Hall school. An early client was Odette Sansom Churchill, who had received the George Cross for her work with the French Resistance; she also designed and painted canvases for the Princess Royal and for the grandmother of Prince Rainier of Monaco (a handbag for use at his wedding to Grace Kelly in 1956). She translated drawings by the wife of Fred Zimmerman into cushions, and was invited to the premiere of his film *A Man for All Seasons* as a result, and among others with whom she worked in London were Mrs Hubert Humphrey – with two secret servicemen – and Lena Horne, whom Rozanne had already met while a student at the Royal College. Clearly, she had sufficient grace to manage these encounters well, but even when she no longer lived with him, her husband's constant belittling never left some recess of her mind. Between his view of her, and the reflection of her professional abilities seen elsewhere, there was too great a dissonance for easy resolution.

LEFT Collage of memorabilia documenting Rozanne and Mathew's life from c.1963–67 and her work for the WHI and American Needlework Center, including her only extant example of crewelwork, made c.1965 in America, a drawing by Mathew and a photograph of him and friend on the Chase's estate in Virginia.

Briefly teaching again in Brighton (at one stage on the college steps, during the protests of the period), in 1968 she applied for a full-time lectureship at Battersea College of Education, which only two years earlier had been validated by the University of London Institute of Education to offer a Bachelor of Education degree. On the morning of her interview she received news that her husband had committed suicide. Working full time – from 1969 as a Senior Lecturer – thus gave her that welcome measure of security, and the opportunity to build a new network of friends, which included colleagues such as the ceramicist Ian Canning and the painter Maggie Lillford, whose oil of Rozanne and gouache of Brian number among her treasured possessions. Equally welcome were the chances to once again 'tread the boards' in the pantomimes put on by her faculty of art, which was based in Manresa House, Roehampton, with a beautiful setting in grounds running into Richmond Park. Such bright moments became a lifeline, like the text ribbons in her current work. Her love of the written word parallels her urge to sculpt, and the results, as in *Orpheus*, demonstrate both elements. The story is in the work. And who might Orpheus represent? We might guess Àsgeir, the misogynist decapitated by the Bacchantes, but the truth is far different, and belongs to another chapter in Rozanne's life.

TOP *Rozanne Hawksley*, oil, 1984–85. Painted by Margaret Lillford, who taught with Rozanne at Manresa House during the 1970s.

ABOVE *Brian Hawksley*, gouache, signed and dated by Margaret Lillford, 1980.

RIGHT & OVERLEAF *Orpheus*, 2006, detail and entire.

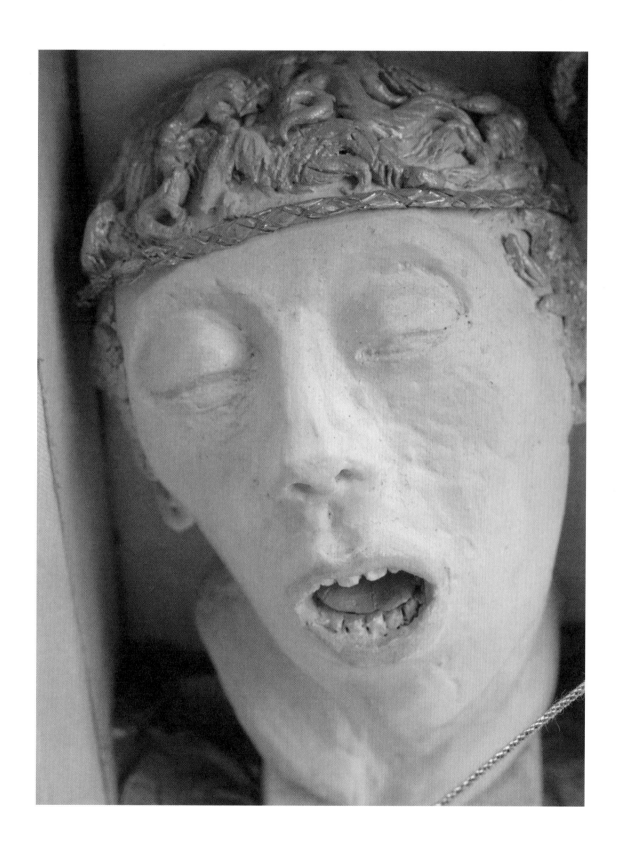

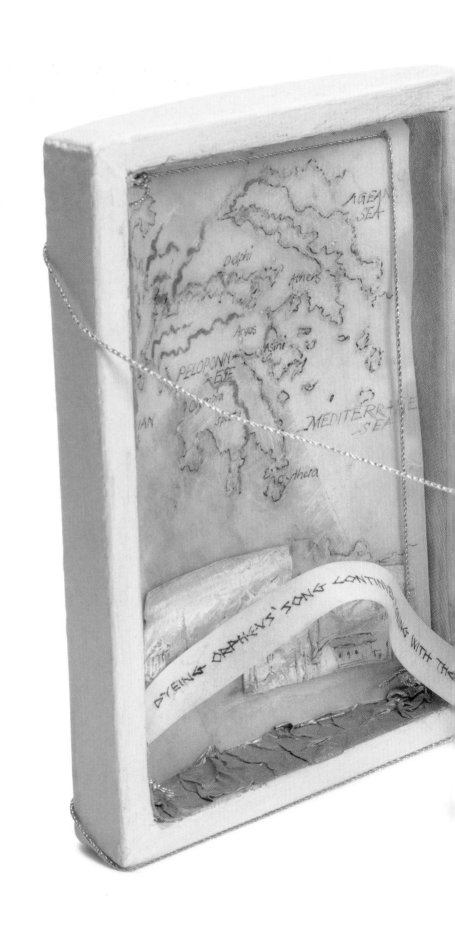

INTO A FUGUE

Looking back on her life as Mrs Scott, Rozanne describes herself as in the wrong boat, on the wrong sea. This choice of metaphor for a life adrift in unfamiliar territory encapsulates a childhood immersion in seafaring as well as a recognition that her own craft, sound though it was, had neither rudder, nor oars. Doing things because she thought that was what one did, was a habit borne out of shyness, out of a fear of being judged and found wanting. Still inclined to a preference for privacy today, she nevertheless now 'believes utterly in the work.' This change began while studying with David Green, a senior lecturer at Goldsmiths College (from 1973–78) who had also built up a successful career as a freelance textile designer, curator, writer and advisor to the BBC since his receipt of the DesRCA in 1965. His skills, enthusiasm and imaginative approach were apparent when she attended his three week summer school in 1975. When he subsequently persuaded her to apply for the Advanced Diploma in Textiles, 'I thought *somebody* had said I'm good at *something*.' His validation was a turning point, or perhaps more aptly, a counterpoint, to the capriccios and fantasias that had increasingly come to haunt Rozanne's sense of self.

Her 'fugues' did not conform to what today is a specific psychiatric condition, dissociative fugue, which describes the temporary but complete loss of identity and travel to a location where a new identity can be adopted. Nevertheless, a flight from self was manifest in the episodes that Rozanne recalls as like being asleep with her eyes open, incapable of movement or speech, for above all the fugue state is a means of self-preservation, by giving respite from intolerable stress. How could such a pressing need for escape have come to be? After all, her cruel first husband was now some six years dead, and she had since enjoyed teaching at Manresa House, then known as the best art education department in England.[1] She had spent her initial year, with the support of Bert Isaac, Head of the Art Department, developing an interdisciplinary approach to the fashion and costume curriculum, one that enfolded music and theatre. With relish, she had worked with Roger Jerome, an English tutor for Manresa House who set up the Theatre Course there (and is now known in the United States for his performances as Charles Dickens). During their second year, students worked with both tutors on a theatrical project, including those with an art elective otherwise studying home economics at a sister campus in Clapham Common. Rozanne recalls one among the latter wanting time off to attend a workshop given by the mime artist, Lindsay Kemp, to which she said, 'of course, go, as long as you bring it back into your work', an echo of what she appreciated in Isaac, a quiet man who when presented with a new idea that he thought could work, would say, 'prove it, prove it, but go ahead and *do* it.'

Her initiatives at Manresa House did not come to fruition without some controversy. The staff at Clapham Common, she recalls, were 'in horror in the first term regarding the pantomime costumes and behaviour.'

PREVIOUS *Veterans*, 1978, ranging from 5cm to 15cm in height. Four from a larger group of wax and clay sculpted figures, bound in gauze and painted.

LEFT Negative of the drawing, *Springfield Summer: self-portrait*, 1977.

To make matters worse, some among them were even less pleased on the occasion when Rozanne's role as Principal Boy called for the line, 'I stand for all that's righteous, good and kind', and all the students stood up and cheered. These events brought back joyful memories of self-confidence while participating in plays and reviews at the Royal College and with the London Artists' Theatre productions (a semi-professional company), resulting in an invitation to a professional audition received too late to act upon it. The missed opportunity left the lingering question: 'what if?'

Yet through the same Manresa amateur dramatics she had met Betty Hawksley, who introduced Rozanne to her brother-in-law, the actor Brian Hawksley. This had been in 1970, when he was performing in the debut of *Vivat! Vivat Regina!* at Chichester Festival Theatre, the Tony-nominated play written by Robert Bolt for his wife, Sarah Miles. Others in the cast were Judy Parfitt and Eileen Atkins. Hawksley played the Bishop of Durham then, as well as when it was brought into London and again in another season at Birmingham Repertory Theatre. He 'loved words, eschewed first night parties, and didn't do the "darling thing", just as Rozanne hated the "fashion thing"'. The romance blossomed and they married on 17th July, 1971. She was 41 and he, ten years older, the first man she was sure she really loved.

All, however, was not easy. What followed was a phase of life recognisable to many women, or rather, several phases collapsed into a period of three to four years.

By 1975 she had experienced the later-marriage phenomena: 'granny', her mother-in-law, in situ for a year or so, with a bad heart and unwilling to draw her pension; the death of Rozanne's father followed shortly by that of her mother, who had suffered for eighteen months with a brain tumour; the unhappiness this caused for her son, Mathew, boarding at Christ's Hospital; and the conflicting joy for Mat, aged 18 in 1976, who was building his own life and would no longer make much use of the room that Brian had done up for the boy, whom he'd come to love as his own son. Overlaid was the early-marriage experience: living at first in a rented flat in Thames Ditton followed by the purchase of a two-up, two-down in Burmester Road along from the Co-op funeral parlour and near Wimbledon Dog Track, a 'tiny run down place with an outside loo and a cold water tap', where they lived in the front room while Brian carried out remarkable renovations, and where she miscarried the child much wanted by them both. The first of the fugues appeared. Finally, there was the reality of her own mid-life career. Brian's remuneration never equalled his considerable talents – he was a fine photographer as well as actor – and although Rozanne was 'only a teacher' to granny, the teacher was supporting them all.

By 1974, she was also teaching in the evenings. In addition to her work in the classroom, she was examining too. In this way she came to know a fellow examiner, Constance Howard, who in 1948 had founded the Embroidery

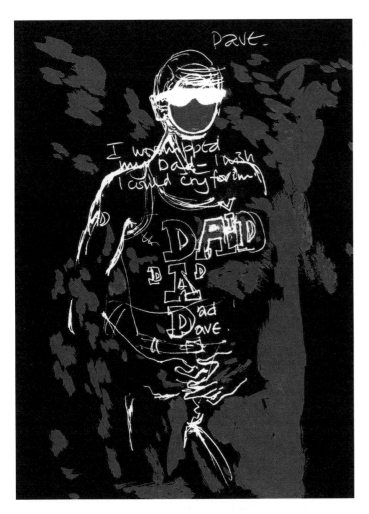

Department at Goldsmiths College, London, and had long been at its helm by the time she was approaching retirement in the summer of 1975.[2] Rozanne mentioned that she knew there was something she needed to find, 'but what?' The reply had pointed her to Green's summer course, and during it she discovered the 'what' and was sure that this was the direction she must take. 'I fought like mad to have the entitled study day off from the senior lectureship at Manresa House, and so every Thursday David Green let me sneak in through the back door of the print room where I worked hard and happily.' Meanwhile, she had applied for the Advanced Diploma and with Bert Isaac's support obtained a sabbatical for the 1976–77 academic year. But as that year progressed, the fugues increased in number. Like the holiday flu or the weekend migraine, the respite from so much responsibility and pressure triggered dark moments. There followed several years in which the fugues and her artistic journey were closely intertwined. During the summer of 1977, for example, she became a day patient at Springfield University Hospital in Tooting, and found herself wandering the nearby graveyard taking photographs and while on the ward, observing the people around her, and later drawing them from memory. These drawings were made into negatives and printed, toile-like, during the 1977–78 academic year, the last undertaken with Green, who had accepted a teaching position in Australia. Prior to his departure Rozanne's fugues had worsened and there was a short and terrifying period when she was warded at Springfield; yet he had ensured that a place was held open for her to complete the diploma. Also a day patient briefly in the autumn of 1978 in the imposing Victorian setting of Atkinson Morley Hospital, Wimbledon, it would be 1980 before she completed what was a two-year course (if taken part-time).

LEFT *Graveyard in Tooting*, 1977.
Photograph by Rozanne Hawksley.
ABOVE *Please look after Mr. Syd*, detail.
Photograph by Brian Hawksley.
OVERLEAF *Please look after Mr. Syd*, 1978, boxed screenprint.

The work she completed during these years included experiments with photography, both as a means of representation and as a process, resulting in a number of haunting self-portraits. Photographs could spark other work, such as *Please look after Mr Syd*, which in encapsulating references to others, was a significant step after her period in Springfield: 'it's the first piece of work that knowingly left me alone and I concentrated on someone else.' This someone else was pictured in *The Evening Standard*, and was 'an elderly man who begged for his patch of South East London to be saved. Mr Syd is saying of his square of houses, surrounding a garden with allotments, "This is all going to be pulled down – what is going to happen to us? The only place I shall be going to is Nunhead cemetery".' Knowing this concern was multiplied over and over again across the city, she did the drawing of Mr Syd and printed it with David Green, who taught her how to introduce colour on it. It remained flat for several years until her urge to work in three-dimensions directed her final treatment of the print, during her last year, when she framed it in a crude fashion with rotten wood – referencing the rubbish and rubble, the conflicting sympathy and cruelty also apparent to her in her own environment. The first piece of stitching done unbidden also started under Green,

and was a now-dismantled piece composed, in the manner of *Mr Syd*, of a rough 'window' with torn lace curtains, behind which were heads made of wadding covered with nylon, with their stitched features a three-dimensional response to the Springfield drawings. (Her first steps into the world of *avant garde* embroidery began later with this piece, when it was accepted by the Embroiderers' Guild for their exhibition at the Commonwealth Institute, London, in 1980 or 1981.) This work was followed by *Bride of Death* and *Wide Sargasso Sea*, which are in some respects as autobiographical as are her self-portrait photographs, created using a method she discovered for herself while working in the darkroom. A group of bandaged figures entitled *Veterans* was made just prior to her most severe breakdown; created in a corner of the print room allocated to her alone, they epitomise her intense compassion for the anguished, heightened by her own experiences. Her Diploma show statement explained: 'An important part of my work has been the drawings done whilst at a psychiatric hospital and my early fascination with the glimpses of the tragic, "mad" first Mrs Rochester in *Jane Eyre*. About twelve years ago I came across *Wide Sargasso Sea* by Jean Rhys, who, similarly fascinated, had written the story of the first Mrs Rochester.'

RIGHT *Self-portraits*, c.1978, photographic experiments.

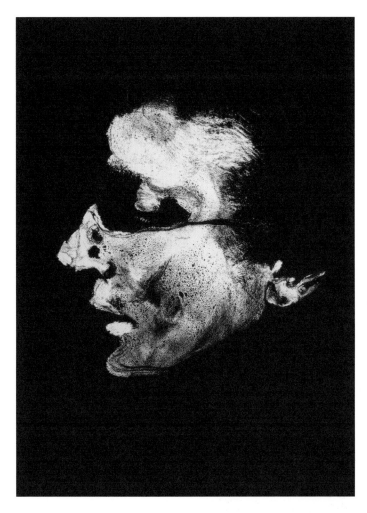
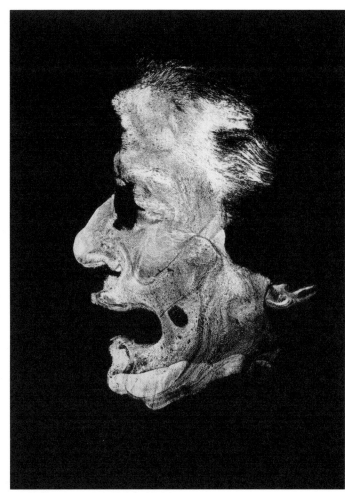
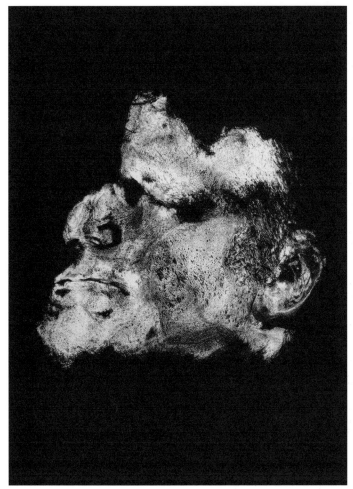
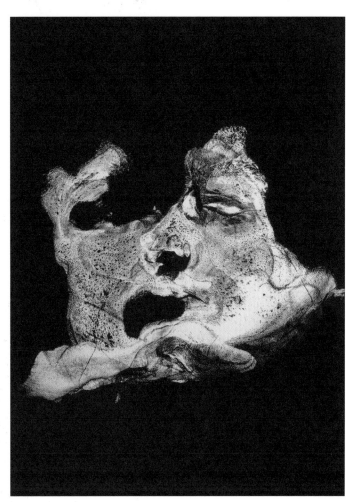

A sympathetic witness for Rozanne's emerging *oeuvre* had been Eirian Short, one of the part-time tutors on the Diploma course and a long-established member of the department whose first training had been in sculpture and who had studied embroidery with Constance Howard more than twenty years before. As Rozanne recalls, 'we got talking because our mothers had both died near enough to each other. We were chatting away and she was understanding of the fact that I'd been in Springfield for the summer. As she was wont to do, she brought a piece of work in that she was working on and showed it to us. And I said, "I know where that is!", which was strange, because in fact it was just a clump of trees. Now a clump of trees, there must be thousands of them all over the UK. And then she said, "oh well, it's on the way to west Wales." "Oh yes", I said. And I have to say at this point I'd been having very very strange dreams of me as a child when I was evacuated, going in and out of woods, clumps of woods, and I looked at this, and I said, "it's at a place called Abercamlais, isn't it?" And she said, "yes, between Senny Bridge and Brecon…" and I said "yes, I was evacuated there" (the second place I was evacuated to) "and I remember that clump of trees very very clearly and I'm having strange dreams about going in and out of it." So, that became a sort of link and Eirian's always been very supportive, as has her husband Denys.' Equally, Rozanne also had the support of Audrey Walker, who had replaced Constance Howard as head of the department. 'How lucky I was that I was always welcomed back, a place kept for me despite the necessary absences.'

On the completion of her diploma, Rozanne became a part-time tutor at Goldsmiths, spared any conflict of loyalty to her former head, Bert Isaac, because in 1979 Manresa House had been closed. She had already been recognised as 'open-minded and responsive to her fellow students' aspirations'[3] and, as Eirian Short put it, 'when her course came to an end, there was no question of letting her go.'[4]

Rozanne remained at Goldsmiths until 1987, during which time she made the first version of *Pale Armistice*, in 1984, and a year later had *Bride of Death* selected for a 62 Group exhibition that toured Japan. She also undertook some work for Brian's brother, Michael, who after working for Gala and Mary Quant Cosmetics, set up his own firm, Cariad Products, in New York. When he relaunched 'Molinard de Molinard' in a replica of the original c.1925 Lalique flacon, Rozanne suggested it be sent to the top buyers with the addition of a silk crêpe de Chine necktie scarf, hand-printed with a frieze of nude women adapted from Lalique's glass. Jane Wildgoose, then a technician in the print department, helped dye the silk peach; the image was screen-discharged to cream; the edges hand-rolled. When more were needed urgently, Rozanne flew to New York with the drawing for the screen and in the space of three days found the fabrics, printer, boxes and wrapping, changing the image to peach on cream silk and having the edges machined to save costs. Much as she enjoyed this sort of challenge, the exhibitions, and the teaching, she had also been dealing with treatments for a kidney tumour for three years during this same period. Finally Brian – aged 66 – needed surgery too and, with his work drying up and the knowledge of a house in Wales for sale, they moved there so that she could finally focus entirely on her own work.

In Pembrokeshire, she also joined an established group of friends, including the Shorts and – ultimately – Audrey Walker, who, looking back on those Goldsmiths' days, observes that: 'For Roz these years were difficult but crucial, and for us we were allowed to realise more fully what a very special artist she is – a person of great sensitivity, tenacious and determined to never compromise as she strives to give material form to her deepest feelings.'[5] In many respects the move to Pembrokeshire was a return to some peace, a point of hope, with a supportive network. Bert Isaac and his wife also lived not far away, and he too knew her as 'a natural teacher of great sensitivity with the capacity to infect students with her own enthusiasm.'[6] For despite her often serious subject matter, there always remains a fine humour and sense of the ridiculous, or, as former student James Hunting recalls, 'she was among the more ironic amongst the tutors, able to see the amusing side of one's work without belittling the serious and important within.' Describing his time at Goldsmiths, during the mid-1980s, as the 'beginning of the rip and stitch' era, he appreciated that she 'never made my work seem frivolous or merely decorative. ...having Rozanne's input then has made me the artist I try to be today, and I will always remember the conversations about hair jewellery, trinkets, scary Scottish partridge claw brooches, and the relative success of my stumpworked mango on a devoré tray (I kid you not, and yes it was as kitsch as you can imagine).' Of his subsequent work as a freelance embroiderer for Givenchy, Julien McDonald and others, he adds, '...and the knowledge of Roz's work in fashion made it easier (mentally anyway) to go in that direction two years after finishing the degree.'[7]

Her diploma show statement had concluded, 'I cannot see an end to my work. Its immediate direction seems to be a drive to explore various images one beneath the other – the "destruction" of the body within the decaying fabrics of life and death.' True to that observation, she has continued to utilise gauze bandages or bindings, as in *Jesus (universal martyr)*, which she describes as long-in-the-making, but completed in 2008. She also continues to use found materials, such as the fractured tile that forms the ground for *Venice*, 2002–03. These are both from a group of objects examining a certain kind of Catholicism, a questioning that also originates from the days of her fugues.

Rozanne herself had started to convert in the early 1960s, and Brian was devout (and pleased, as a result, that Manresa House had once been a Jesuit retreat where one of his favourite poets, Gerard Manley-Hopkins, had taught Classics in the 1870s). Having considered joining a brotherhood when younger, Brian had become a conscientious objector and Rozanne fondly remembers a clever, handsome, gentle man, 'Teddy tum tum', as the young Mathew called his much-loved step-father. 'A safe place.' But he was unable to use his faith to embrace the torn realities of living, and never found a way to strike a comfortable balance between duty and a lust for life.

ABOVE *Venice*, 2002–03. The fractured piece of tile was collected with Brian while in Venice, and the piece composed after he died.

RIGHT *Jesus (universal martyr)*, completed 2008, detail. This work was over ten years in the making.

Often, when speaking of the late 1970s, Rozanne returns to the fact that David Green had understood her references to her 'fugues' and how, when she was in such a state of mind, he would call her Roxanny and invite her into his office off the print room to listen to Vivaldi. The language of the musical form, fugue, is well suited to an understanding of both her attitude to her work and its final form. There is no simple, singular and progressive development; instead the *fugato* approach that was established then, developed itself thereafter as themes have been iterated, overlapping through the passing years. Each composition is contrapuntal and begins, perhaps, with a questioning of religion, a fascination with women's destiny, or the tender observation of human suffering; thoughts are given voice through found objects, a sort of rubble in which things are nevertheless not 'out of their place' nor, by allusion, 'out of their mind'. In the long, very long gestation period of many pieces, some are substantially remade (or re-born), just as in the musical form, when new passages are developed from previously heard material. In music, these are called 'episodes', an additional if diversionary parallel to the psychological fugue state.

More to the point in the case of Rozanne's *fugato* style is her use of text in her work, since it is so often text designed to be spoken. Thus, her making of *King Lear*

– in which are the lines '...so we'll live, and pray, and sing, and tell old tales and laugh at gilded butterflies...'[8] – began in 1976 when reading it aloud sharpened her recognition of madness. Kimono-shaped (and inspired by her husband's wearing of Japanese shoes around the garden, in preparation for a role), it is composed from her first printed textiles, for which Rozanne drew directly through the printing-screen barrier with a knife to make the imagery. It lay unfinished, although prompting her to create two later pieces, now perished, incorporating butterflies. As an example of 'themes and variations', it is now part of an installation underway for 2009, which includes a panel printed with the passage, above, from *Lear*. Among other works prompted by the spoken word is *For Brian: our revels now are ended*, in which at first little words were stitched on a black ribbon; then, while she was convalescing from a hysterectomy after Brian's death 'it sort of started to grow, the black glove, the wedding ring, a crown for a king or clown, and shards of text as spoken by Prospero in Brian's recording of *The Tempest*: "Our revels now are ended. These our actors as I foretold you, were all spirits and are melted into air, into thin air... We are such stuff as dreams are made on, and our little life is rounded with a sleep".'[9] In her incorporation of aural clues, and especially evident in pieces relating to Brian's roles, she provides an exquisitely effective metaphorical marriage between her work and her life.

LEFT *King Lear*, unfinished kimono made of screen-printed cotton drill and organdie, 1976.

OVERLEAF *For Brian: our revels now are ended*, 2006–07, detail.

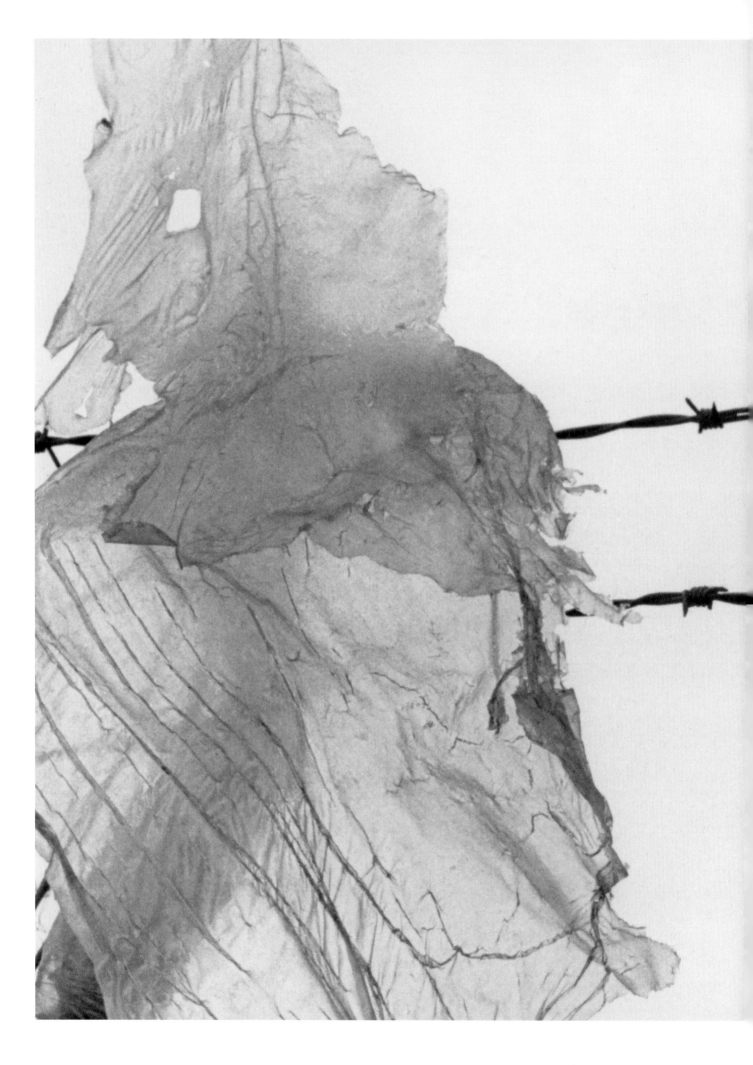

A Dark Line Runs Through It

Consider the topic, 'line', from every angle and it becomes clear how central it is to Rozanne Hawksley's work. In her teaching, a former student, Su Duncombe Bull, says: 'The course at Goldsmiths was very free and Roz emphasised that although it was most important to have a free spirit and imagination, it was important to pay attention to detail in the execution of a project... She was always so avidly interested and encouraging in all aspects of the work I was doing with an all round approach – suggesting artists and areas for research, guiding but not pushing, gently extending the boundaries. She was also very good on technical advice for dealing with textiles. Whenever I cut a line in fabric I think of her as she impressed on me the importance of precision when you are working, that a line cut in fabric should be as precise as a drawn line.'[1]

As the passage above suggests, it is the precision of a cut line that determines the sculptural success or failure of a garment, or indeed, of any assembly of materials. Line, then, describes a three-dimensional possibility as well as, in the cutting of toiles, the outer edge or perimeter. Then too, it is analogous to an essential element of both sewing and shipping: the thread and the rope being distinguished only by their diameter, from thin to thick. Finally, it can be used in drawing to build up texture, shading and contours. In all of these ways and more, she has developed a mastery of line that underpins the diversity of her output. She is very aware of the advantages arising from her training: 'I feel very lucky that I was one of a generation of grant-given art students whose courses valued drawing – drawing for every reason and purpose, and if later we rejected one purpose we knew why. I still love it, value it and thank heaven for it.'

Rozanne's background and training has produced a keen eye for 'found' lines, those that can be observed in city and country, inland and by the sea. These appear most evidently in a series of photographic studies made while a student at Goldsmiths in the late 1970s. In these she observed barbed wire ensnaring a swirling mass of discarded plastic wrapping. The composition captures the tension between the material that would be free and the barbed and twisted metal strands that served as its accidental captor. In *Glove on a wire*, part of an installation staged some dozen years later in Wales, she deliberately evoked this metaphor for entrapment as a response to a trip to Łódź, in Poland, where alongside the WWII German concentration camp for men were two more, one for women – who made the striped clothing for prisoners – and another for children, who made shoes. The setting for this piece was the field beyond the garden of Eirian and Denys Short, in Wales, where Network, a small group of sculptors in west Wales, were exhibiting. By that time, one-time tutor and then colleague Eirian had come to know Rozanne well, the two also having shown together for some years with the 62 Group, with the Embroiderers' Guild and elsewhere, both within and beyond Pembrokeshire. Eirian recalls 'watching her development from the first tentative beginnings of little bandaged figures to her monumental installations today. Her work has never been less than compassionate and moving, with a fine attention to detail and immaculate execution. In a medium in which it is easy to be seduced by decorative qualities and clever techniques, Roz's work has always carried a message.'[2]

The theme of barbed wire also appears in a series of very small quilted panels into which she has incorporated line in several ways. These exercises in stitch, also made during her studentship at Goldsmiths, record her then rough, run-down environment. With stitched representations of graffiti as well as barbed wire, the quilting is deliberately unkempt to capture the unease induced by grim surroundings. That the work is consciously untidy is highlighted by comparison to illustrations Rozanne completed at the same time, for Eirian Short's book, *Quilting: Technique, design and application*, which was published by Batsford in January 1979. Here is precision again, of a different sort, invoked

in order to give clear and helpful instructions. They also illustrate just how conscientious Rozanne was, for they were undertaken during a period of fugues, done when she 'came out of unreality at about 6pm and I could draw for two hours.' It is tempting to see these as representative of a 'bottom line', a foundation of skill that never faltered even in her darkest moments. This point is reinforced by the advice she passed on to her students, among them Victoria Brown, who was tutored by Rozanne while at Goldsmiths from 1980–84 and again when at the RCA, from 1984–87: 'She drummed it into me that whatever happened outside the studio should not impact on my work and that the work would carry me through and that was something I should not relinquish...'.

Like many other former students, Victoria Brown also recalls elements that are often hidden in Rozanne's work: her passion for fabric, her savouring of details of their construction, and the importance of

ABOVE *Jesus Saves with the Woolwich* and *Sophocles rules ok,* quilted croquis, 1978–80. Two of several small samples.

RIGHT 'Suggestions for quilted accessories', from *Quilting: Technique, design and application* by Eirian Short, published by Batsford in January 1979.

OVERLEAF *There is No Water...*, c.2007, detail. The inscription, from T.S. Eliot's poem, *The Waste Land*, reads 'There is no water but only rock, Rock and no water, There is not even solitude in The Mountains.'

selecting the right stitch for each purpose: 'She is also a stickler for craftsmanship and wouldn't let a poor or badly-stitched seam go... nor would she tell you either, you just knew you had to do it right for her.' For Victoria's work with felt, Rozanne taught her the herringbone stitch, which she now uses often. It not only reminds her of her former tutor, but is also used 'in homage' to her. 'One of my own students pointed out that I am always showing students herringbone stitch too (and I too wax lyrical about the beauty in its functionality). ...Roz's teaching has not only influenced me as a maker and given me a life-long confidence in making, process and truth to one's work and self, she has also influenced me as a teacher and lecturer... she had the real gift of sharing her enthusiasm for life and her work and making that sense of enquiry embed itself in each of us who have worked with her.'[3] Rozanne's teaching thus not only moved concepts of embroidery away from its definition as solely decorative, and towards

a much greater appreciation of its utilitarian role, but also contributed to the emphasis now placed on another sort of line: the line of enquiry. That point of attack, the belief that art can arise from pursuing ones particular interests, however unusual or seemingly unfashionable, came from years of experience, and was already evident during her years at Manresa House, where from 1967–70 one student was Penny Lucas. Discovering in 2008, through a photograph on the internet, that her Mrs Scott was now Rozanne Hawksley, she wrote, '...it was more than the transference of knowledge that had an impact on me. It was the fact that you treated us as individuals and found time for us all; you encouraged us to value ourselves, our work and our opinions.'[4]

As lines of enquiry go, if laid and cross-couched thread denotes barbed wire in an evident way, the attenuated, tensioned threads seen in works such as *Look on small beautiful things* (1990 ongoing) make far more subtle reference to utilitarian lashing.

accessories

145 Suggestions for quilted accessories. Rozanne Hawksley. The travel bag, make-up bag and spectacle case are made up in transparent PVC with quilted bindings.

134

The delicate silk and gold threads pinion bones in place, rendering them like rare specimens to be studied, classified and admired. The same technique is incorporated into *Pale Rider*, of 2008, its skull and crossed bones giving a more direct clue to the actual inspiration for the surrounding gold threads, for they refer to the shrouds, or main ropes, that secure the mast on a traditional square-rigged ship. The complexity of the glove, with its additional allusions to the ceremonial garb that – like shrouds – might equally obscure, disguise or become dress for burial, contrasts sharply with the simplicity of the individually mounted bones, a point

emphasised by Eirian Short: 'While she rejoices in the use of silks, laces, jewels, bones and metal threads, she is equally eloquent working on plain calico...'.[5] In both cases, however, the threads are also pure lines, that is, standing for a mark made by pen or pencil. Not that there ever existed a drawing for any of these pieces. Rozanne explains: 'Put simply, if I had drawn it I would have done it, emotionally and intellectually. Therefore making it would be a mere translation – a pointless exercise – leaving no room for the selection of materials (I use this term in its widest meaning) as the piece progresses... for the element of chance is important to me.'

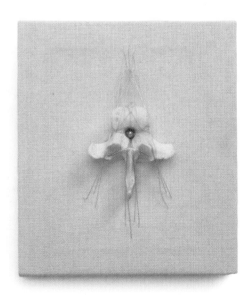 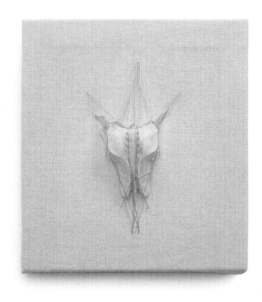

ABOVE *Look on small beautiful things*, an on-going series begun in the 1990s. Two canvas panels with thread-pinioned bones; from a large set.
RIGHT *Pale Rider*, glove, 2008.

For Rozanne, there is a clear demarcation between her drawing books and her sketches in notebooks, the latter 'small and scrappy, indecipherable other than to me, unless technical directions or constructional thoughts... I suppose that the cluttered attic space that is my workroom is also a full-scale working notebook – a reference space. To anyone else it probably seems a horrifying tip. To me nothing is irrelevant: the floor, tables, work bench, tea chests, jars, bottles, boxes all full, the floor littered with references that have excited, horrified or moved me.' The drawings in the notebooks are noticeably lacking in feeling, being intended to catch the details 'to add to the emotional and visual mind-stored references.' The notations, purely for information, include considered studies that record, for example, the articulation of a particular neck muscle and its relationship to the angle of the lower jaw in a certain position. She has owned more than one copy of *Gray's Anatomy* since her days at the art college in Portsmouth,

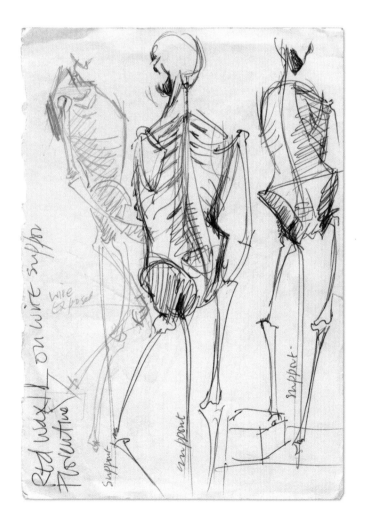

and many hours have been spent pouring over other medical source material for sketches ranging from those of a surgeon's equipment and stitches, or wounds and bandaging, to anatomical models including those for the instruction of midwives. Other sketches might be encountered objects, such as the reliquaries sketched hastily in Seville in 1989, during the few moments when these could be seen during Holy Week. When included in *Creating Sketchbooks for Embroiderers and Textile Artists*, in 2005, the author, Kay Greenlees,

used these 'quick, dynamic drawings and annotations' to exemplify 'a clear example of work that involves an ongoing internal dialogue [about] serious and difficult issues... not immediately visual...'.[6] Rozanne herself continues, 'often these can have been noted months or even years before I have the strong feeling that I must make whatever it is, that is, the subject of the notation, or rather, to try to externalise three-dimensionally that *response* to the subject.'

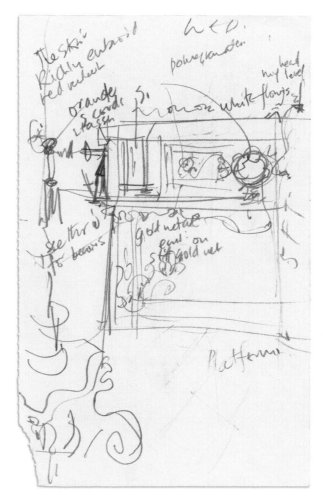

She does of course draw to answer the needs of a commission, but her croquis or constructive sketches are always presented with the proviso that there exists room for change. This was the case with the *Mitre* commissioned by the Worshipful Company of Weavers in 1996, to celebrate its chaplain, the Rt Revd. Rt Hon. Richard Chartres, becoming Bishop of London. Writing of the project three years later, she noted that 'much of my time was spent in research drawing and hard thinking before I was able to submit a design in which I believed absolutely.' Incorporating an array of symbols and imagery to reflect the Bishop's 'faith, his interest in the arts and sciences, his scholarship and his links with the Eastern Orthodox Church' as well as the already noted 'continuing interest in the world's philosophies and beliefs,'[7] at the base of a cross of bones is a depiction of the walled City of London. The marks were drawn, painted and stitched – some on fine old gloving leather, the shapes cut, padded and applied with couching using gold-claret[8] and gold fine cord with silk thread. And while close to the working drawing, changes were made as the work progressed. The Bishop, for his part, appreciated 'such a wealth of symbolism within a strong and coherent overall design', giving way to humour when adding that he would wear it with confidence, 'knowing that I am not subscribing to the ersatz gaudiness... school of ecclesiastical millinery nor to [that of] deadening blandness.'[9]

ABOVE *Mitre for the Bishop of London,* working drawing, 1996.
RIGHT Views of Rozanne's studio.

A self portrait

June '07.

Entirely different are the drawing books, of which there are dozens. These are private reflections of her own state of mind, each being 'an entity in itself – it exists as a drawing only – and each is my decided response at that time to a situation or a search for a resolution, that is, purely to resolve a feeling.' Few have seen these drawings until now. Among the handful who have are Philip Hughes, Director of Ruthin Craft Centre – whose response was the question, 'could she be described as [a] contemporary "Goya"...?'[10] – and Andrew Salmon, Director of Creative Exhibitions and owner of several of Rozanne's works, including a set of ten of the self-portraits, the only ones to have left her studio from among the thousands that she has drawn. Asked why he wanted to purchase these along with other pieces, his response was unhesitating: 'technical brilliance, yes, but above all, the content... she is *the* undiscovered real talent in textiles today.'[11]

LEFT & ABOVE *Self-portraits* of various dates, from Rozanne's private drawing books.

The technical brilliance might easily be overlooked, particularly in an assemblage such as *Queen of Spades* (2008). Only close study reveals that the cards splayed out from the gloved 'hand' are not derived from a purchased deck, but drawn and painted by Rozanne herself. On vellum, not just cardboard, they are rendered with several shades of black and brown inks to produce a seemingly mutating image, and done so because the story she is recounting calls for it. Only by that means could she suggest that the last card, the uppermost, is changing from the Ace of Spades to the Queen of Spades, the climactic event in the short story, *The Queen of Spades*, written by Alexander Pushkin in 1834. In this tale of a wealthy Countess who won back a lost fortune through success at the card table, the plot turns around a young Russian officer who seduces her beautiful niece, intent on gaining the Countess's riches.

As she dies (an event brought about by the seducer) she tells him her secret, naming the significant cards: the Three, Seven and Ace of Spades, each played in turn within 24 hours of each other. Successful on the first two evenings, on the third he triumphantly plays the Ace of Spades, but as he does, it is transformed into the Queen. He has lost everything. The tale is well known, having inspired an opera by Tchaikovsky, and several films, most importantly for Rozanne, a 1949 film directed by Thorold Dickinson and starring Edith Evans, Yvonne Mitchell and Anton Walbrook. 'It was a talking point for years in the 1950s, beautifully shot in black and white, and there is a moment where the young officer (Walbrook) looks into the coffin where the Countess lies dead and she opens her eyes and winks – and I've never forgotten it.' Looking at the card again, one can see the Queen with one eye closed, winking.

ABOVE *Queen of Spades*, glove, 2008, detail. Showing the painted vellum card at the moment of its transformation from an Ace to a Queen of Spades.

RIGHT *Cogita Mori: think on death*, brisé fan, painted vellum on wood, 1999. Reading from right to left are, in Latin, the words of De Profundis: 'from out of the depths have I cried to thee, my God.' The right side is indicative of a desolate or wicked life and descent into hell, the left, evidence of a good life and rewarding death. The winged eye of God looks down on both as our time passes. Translation and further texts are on the reverse.

OVERLEAF *Cogita Mori: think on death*, detail.

This intensity of observational memory, together with the Rozanne's neo-mannerist aesthetic, brings to mind Roger Fry's essay, 'The Artist's Vision', in which he remarks that 'artists always lead the way in awakening a new admiration for forgotten and despised styles, and that in doing so they anticipate both the archaeologist and the collector,' going on to argue that most people look to understand the 'meaning-for-life', but do not see the detail, whereas an artist's vision 'dwells much more consciously and deliberately upon it,' a knack that children have also not yet lost, 'so they look at things with some passion.' Only art, he contends, prompts this kind of seeing in the viewer, and he suspects 'that such an object must be made by someone in whom the impulse was not to please others, but to express a feeling of his own.'[12] This might equally be read in relation to the brisé fan, *Cogita Mori: think on death* (1999). Made of wooden sticks with painted vellum on their upper surface, it was the result of an urge to make a fan for Death, an idea brought into focus when, leaving a church in Bruges, she saw, engraved high up on a wall, a skull looking to its right – the turning away by man from evil – and, at the back, a long grave-digger's spade and scythe. This led to each base of the fan sticks being shaped as a coffin. Reading from right to left are

the words 'de profundis' a reference to the poem written by Oscar Wilde while in prison, roughly translating as 'out of the depths'. The rendering captures the essence of an engraved image, but for the reader of Wilde, its colouration has additional allusions, suggesting as it does his passage: 'For us there is only one season, the season of sorrow. The very sun and moon seem taken from us. Outside, the day may be blue and gold, but the light that creeps down through the thickly-muffled glass of the small iron-barred window beneath which one sits is grey and niggard. It is always twilight in one's cell, as it is always twilight in one's heart.'[13]

Rozanne has read Fry, and also argued on occasion in exam boards about students missing the point when their work was not observant, not enriched with their care, reflection and reading: 'I thought it an insult to throw something together, especially if the topic was controversial, because the core was then missing, making it a bagatelle.' In contrast, her work is always mediated by a depth of understanding, whether the subject is as 'small' as a single dreaded death, or as large as the slaughter of many. That understanding, while so often associated with a memory of a visual or aural stimulus, is equally dependent for its externalisation on her ability to draw, whether with thread, as notations, or to exorcise an emotion.

THE HUMAN CONDITION

Gaza
Egypt
Vietnam
Korea Se
Klands

At first glance, Rozanne Hawksley's work can be viewed as if partaking of coalesced opposites: large versus small, public versus private; considering honour versus horror. But however disparate the physical manifestation of her art may be, the core is always emotional. 'Too much deliberation at the time is not good,' she says, adding that she strives to keep her response to the topic at hand in an animated state, turning, often, to the written word or music to reinvigorate her sense of excitement, dread and purpose, which in an uneasy alliance, are her motivating forces. Often over the past twenty years her focus has been on war, and by examining this body of work one can see how the triumvirate of dialectic characteristics noted above – essentially scale, ultimate audience, if any, and context – interact to create 'the ambiguity and layers of potential interpretation... essential in a great work.'[1] Like almost all of her pieces, those recording her reactions to conflict have not been made for a specific purpose or venue, with the exception of requests to create for a specific space.

A good starting point is an installation of 1995, made for the Myles Meehan Gallery in Darlington. Stark in its use of a canvas-lidded cage, relieved only by a spotlit orange set inside amid a prisoner's meagre belongings, and a neon strip-light dado on the surrounding walls, it was a reaction to the experience of Brian Keenan, who spent four-and-a-half years as a hostage in Beirut, Lebanon from 11 April 1986 to 24 August 1990. The contents of the cage illuminate a passage from Keenan's own account, which was included in the installation's text panel: 'I lift an orange into the flat, filthy palm of my hand and feel and smell and lick it. The colour orange, the colour, the colour, my God the colour orange.'[2] The title of her installation, *The Colour Orange – a line of hope*, adds further explication, referring to Keenan's ecstasy and his dance of joy in response to the fruit. Yet in its execution other references are present, ones personal to the artist herself: 'I am drawn to the secret, the allegory, a meaning often hidden, secret ritual, that behind the facade. Strong visual memories lurk – the reliquaries and dark waters of Venice; in Seville the small, concentrated gleam of gilt in the barely lit, almost unfathomable interior behind the bright carved exterior of a church: an argument between dark and light.'

Repeatedly, as she takes the viewer to an imagined setting, the effects of conflict on soldier and civilian alike are not so much observed as alluded to, allowing each individual who witnesses the work to step into the shoes of her subjects. Never simply protests against war, they are instead imbued with heartfelt empathy for those who suffer, on whose behalf she has been known to rage at calloused reportage by the press.

PREVIOUS *Mission Accomplished*, 2008, detail.

LEFT *The Colour Orange – a line of hope*, installation at the Myles Meehan Gallery, Darlington, 1995. Photograph courtesy of the Myles Meehan Gallery.

ABOVE *The Colour Orange – a line of hope*, detail showing the contents of the cage. Photograph courtesy of the Myles Meehan Gallery.

Casualties were surprisingly light is one such installation, created for the undercroft in the ruins of the Bishop's Palace, St David's, Pembrokeshire, in 1991. Its seventeen crosses on a grid represent the first seventeen British soldiers killed in the Gulf War, with each cross covered as if with a body-bag, tied and labelled with invented service numbers and the stencilled words, 'via Brize Norton', the RAF airbase where, then as now, the war dead are brought from battlefields abroad. As with every installation, it was composed, in part, in response to the space it occupied. In this case the height of the crosses, so nearly touching the ceiling, suggest the enclosure of the aeroplane in which the bodies had been flown, as well as producing a simile for the narrow-minded journalistic summary of these losses as being of little consequence. This work was subsequently selected for the Łódź Triennial in 1992 and remained in Poland, a donation by Rozanne to the Łódź Central Museum of Textiles.

LEFT & ABOVE *Casualties were surprisingly light*, installation in the undercroft, the Bishop's Palace, St David's Pembrokeshire, 1991, and detail. Photographs by Brian Hawksley.

Similarly, the themes of impersonal or imposing spaces, from prison cells to cathedrals, were brought together in her allusion to the cabinet room or political sanctum, as seen in '...*a treaty will be signed some time today*'. Maggie Grey, then editor of *The World of Embroidery* magazine, saw it in 1997 and devoted much of her September issue's editorial to its impact: "'It is not enough today to make pretty patterns. Embroidery must have something to say – a message to impart." So said Constance Howard in her speech at the opening of the *Art of the Stitch* exhibition. Certainly the exhibits at this wonderful exhibition had plenty to say for themselves but my thoughts returned immediately to an installation work of Rozanne Hawksley that I viewed the week before in a gallery in Swansea. The title of the exhibition was '...*a treaty will be signed some time today*' and the theme was the attention paid to the useless shuffling of papers while lives are lost, children maimed and the horrors of war march on. It wasn't a "nice" experience, this work, but oh it was powerful. The gallery was a recycled church that proved the ideal venue, and the visitors' book contained some very telling comments, proving that the point had been well made.'[3] Of this first showing, in Swansea's Mission Gallery, Rozanne herself notes that 'these "enclosed" spaces, often containing objects, can only be made of significance by the reasoning behind the work and the clinical decision about materials. The white cloth with distinct equally spaced folds – echoes of a strong ritual underlined by the formal piles of white papers waiting at either end of the table and the placing of two black chairs, black pens waiting – was absolutely vital to the message: the disaster of the world's state and its future further

devastation piled in the middle of the table. Over it, out of the darkness a sword was suspended, tipped with blood; around, the sound of time passing.' *Treaty* was shown anew at the Knitting and Stitching Show in the autumn of 2000, which coincided with the unravelling of the peace process in the Middle East. 'It is difficult,' the Show's organiser commented, 'to recall another piece which has had so great an impact on visitors.'[4] While she knows of a friend who has said 'never look at Rozanne Hawksley's work, it's so horrible...', she also met a German women, observing this work and weeping. Rozanne expressed concern, identified herself as the artist and as this woman turned around, seeing they were the same age, they put their arms out to each other. 'That's it exactly, isn't it ridiculous?', the German woman said, and shortly afterwards they worked out that their uncles probably fought each other in the Libyan dessert.

The beginning of an understanding of the impact of places of isolation, reflection or disquiet can be found in a much earlier installation, made many years before with Bert Isaac at Manresa House. A large enclosure made of polished metal panels salvaged from Heathrow and with no apparent agenda, it was nevertheless intended to create an environment in which occupants lost their sense of location. In the summer of 2001, she reflected on a different kind of loss of location, in *Refugee*. In this work, a series of black heavy canvas panels were suspended in one of the several undercrofts at St David's Bishop's Palace. She had deliberately selected what looked like a dungeon. Having looked up various terms for refugee, she stencilled one word on each of the seven lengths, then defacing the central panel alone. This work once again typifies her awareness of the relationship between an installation and the given space, the integration of which 'is of great importance; they hopefully become undifferentiated intellectually, yet emotionally they may work deliberately one against the other – discord – or merge – accord.' Here the discordance between the rugged simplicity of the setting and the vivid graffiti-covered central banner adds to its conveyance of an abhorrence of a violent and intolerant response to asylum seekers.

OPPOSITE '*...a treaty will be signed some time today*', installation, 1997, as shown at the Mission Gallery. Photograph by Nicola O'Neill.

LEFT *Refugee*, installation included in an exhibition of Network, in the undercroft, the Bishop's Palace, St David's Pembrokeshire, 2001. Photograph by Denys Short.

While installations are clearly meant to be seen, Rozanne does not think of how people may interpret her private work while she creates them. Nor does she feel bound to leave a piece alone. For example, *Sir Galahad* began as a testament to those lost and injured on *RFA Sir Galahad,* hit twice during the Falklands War of 1982 and disabled so severely that it had to be sunk subsequently, becoming an official war grave. Among the 48 dead were 32 from the Welsh Guards; among the survivors was Guardsman Simon Weston, who suffered 49 percent burns and whose story was widely reported. Rozanne's own empathy for the courage of the Guards was founded on personal experience as a girl during World War II, when she saw a neighbour of an aunt, on leave from the Navy, whose 'face was red but it was his hands that had been burnt terribly badly.' One of the many times she was ill in hospital after the *Sir Galahad*, she thought of how she would still be able to see and use her hands, as opposed to the survivors who were so crippled. Some time after her recovery, that realisation prompted the making of this piece. Begun in 1987 and left as an exposed, mutilated clay and wax figure on a rough wooden cross for some twenty years, it was veiled in 2008 to indicate her indignation at the lack of public acknowledgment for soldiers returning from Iraq, where the replacement *RFA Sir Galahad* was involved in landing troops in 2003. The veiling also parallels the custom of veiling crosses from Passion Sunday (the fifth Sunday of Lent) until the Resurrection, which was originated 'to create an atmosphere of restraint and simplicity.'[5]

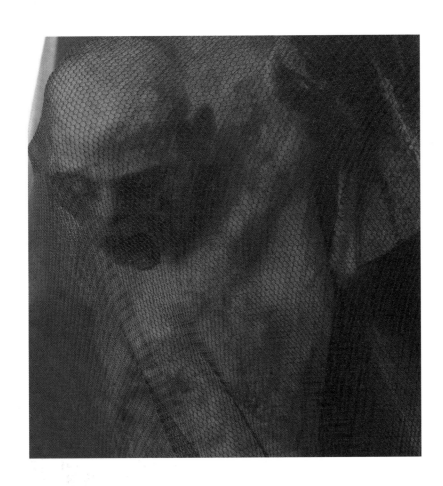

LEFT *Sir Galahad,* begun in 1987, completed in 2008.
ABOVE *Sir Galahad,* detail.

We are legion also began in response to the sacrifices of Welsh soldiers and was first exhibited with *Treaty* in Swansea, in 1997. It was then selected for inclusion in the Arts and Crafts pavilion at the 2002 National Eisteddfod of Wales, a peripatetic annual Welsh arts festival held at St David's in that year. The severed bones, beef because of their weight and comparison to human bones, are set on rough wooden panels, each made uniformly to suggest a military shield. The sawn-through ends are a literal form of butchery, providing the metaphor for slaughter but in addition – when observed with care – sight of the bones' complex calcified structure. This too is a metaphor, a message from Rozanne, who urges us to see the beauty there, just as it can be found in the heart of the mutilated warrior. Look once more, and straight on, and the shanks suggest open mouths, perhaps moaning, or howling with pain. As is often the case, one can find an experience in Rozanne's past that informs the work. Her cousin,

John David Pibworth, was among the Royal Engineers who were dropped behind enemy lines in advance of D-Day, and in the course of laying a bridge for Polish tanks to advance, had his legs shattered by the explosion of a cache of live ammunition. Refusing amputation on the field, both legs were reconstructed by British surgeons using metal rods and monkey's bones. By this time – June 1944 – the thirteen year-old Rozanne recalls that, 'we had by then moved to a little tiny house in Sheet, near Petersfield, which was attached to Uncle Mop and Aunty Daisy's slightly bigger house in which my cousin Stephen also lived, and JD convalesced there.' However, everyone she knew had suffered the results of the bombs aimed at Portsmouth, 18 miles away: 'we had a few sticks of furniture of our own... the piano survived and a sofa and a couple of chairs.' As a result, JD recuperated on her family's sofa, since his own family didn't have one. And it was this same house that Jimmy Clavell visited. Aside from her observation of the many recovering servicemen around about and even more distressed people who were bombed out, this first-hand knowledge of the disabling effects of war bequeathed to her an unflinching gaze that replaced her childhood bewilderment.

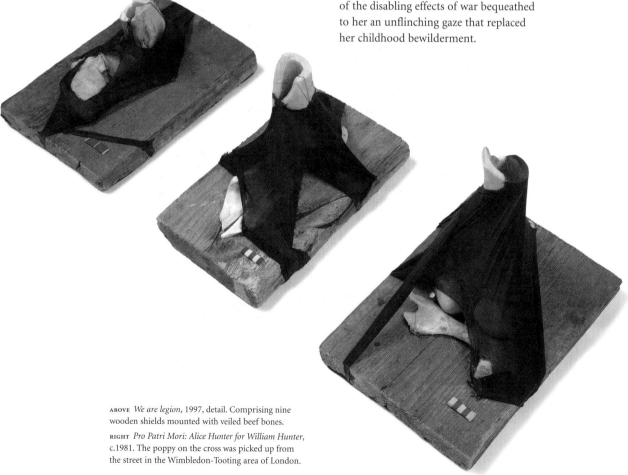

ABOVE *We are legion*, 1997, detail. Comprising nine wooden shields mounted with veiled beef bones.

RIGHT *Pro Patri Mori: Alice Hunter for William Hunter*, c.1981. The poppy on the cross was picked up from the street in the Wimbledon-Tooting area of London.

As in *Sir Galahad*, veiling was used in *We are legion* too. But in the latter it represents the veiled women of the Middle East, equally the victims of war. Also veiled is an even earlier work, of about 1981, entitled *Pro Patri Mori: Alice Hunter for William Hunter*. Its black tulle veiling, overlaying a wreath composed of scraps of Edwardian jet beading, is suggestive of widow's weeds; its title, meaning 'it's so glorious to die for one's country', is the stern solace for bereaved military wives everywhere. In each of these three veiled pieces is evidence of Rozanne's sensitivity to cloth in motion. The crucifix is double veiled with pure silk chiffon, with the underneath layer on the true bias, to form a closer, darker sheath, while the upper layer, arranged at a slightly different angle, creates a translucent covering. Strategically nailed silk chiffon achieves similarly subtle variances of tonality in *Legion*. In the third piece, made in memory of her seamstress grandmother, there is also the suggestion of the covered

mirrors, once part of funereal protocol. In an emblematic fashion, the veiling also brings to mind another form of covering, of the 'make do and mend' sort. Rozanne recounts how her parents transformed two leather bucket car-seats, her father obtaining some little wooden supports and her mother, some cretonne: 'God knows how she got hold of that – down the market or cut-up curtains – to make two chair covers... and we had those car seats until the death of my parents.' Whether for modesty, humility or practicality, the act of veiling or covering is a practice typically handed down from mother to daughter. This adds a tenderness to all three works that is at odds with the sinister connotations of black cloths. Instead, these textiles symbolise three traditional female roles: offering protection against an unsympathetic world, restraint against aggression, and dignity in bereavement, respectively.

He had a bad war like pretty well everyone and his last days were very sad; he ended up beachcombing; he could never settle, he loved being in the Army.' The drawing, done in the early 1990s, imagines his state of mind while in a German prison camp in Poland, where the prisoners worked in a mine and were told it would be flooded if troops arrived to free them. Escaping briefly, he had his hands tortured upon being caught. 'He had been on the Western Front where his rifle apparently froze to his hand; he was at Dunkirk where his mate was shot standing next to him. He was at the second Battle of El Alamein in late 1942 and he wouldn't hear a word said about Montgomery; he said, "he told us straight, he told us everything...".' The Monstrance, a vessel to hold a consecrated Host, was made by Rozanne in 1987 to memorialise Harry's confirmation during that posting in the Libyan desert. In it, Christ is lashed to the cross like a man shot for cowardice, and the sheep's toothy jaw represents the lambs led to slaughter. No belittlement of faith, the handmade nails represent the making of the stigmata, and for this seaman-turned-soldier, are a metonym for Harry's own nailing of his colours to his mast. As he pledged his devotion to his God, this monstrance implies, Harry knew of sacrifices ahead: 'Then he said to them all: "If anyone would come after me, he must deny himself and take up his cross daily and follow me".'[6] It was only some fifteen months later that he was captured in Italy during the Allied forces' Anzio Beachhead operation and sent to Poland.

Both *Halt! Who goes there?* and *Monstrance for a field of battle* were created by Rozanne in memory of Harry, her mother's favourite brother. He had gone to sea as a ship's steward when only 14 or 15 years old and then joined the Grenadier Guards just before the war. 'He must have been very young; he thought "fabulous uniform, the scarlet coats" and that he might be standing in a sentry box.

ABOVE *Halt! Who goes there?*, early 1990s. For Rozanne's Uncle Harry, who had a bad war but still maintained these were the best years of his life. Photograph by Brian Hawksley.

RIGHT *Monstrance for a field of battle*, 1987, detail. Photograph by Brian Hawksley.

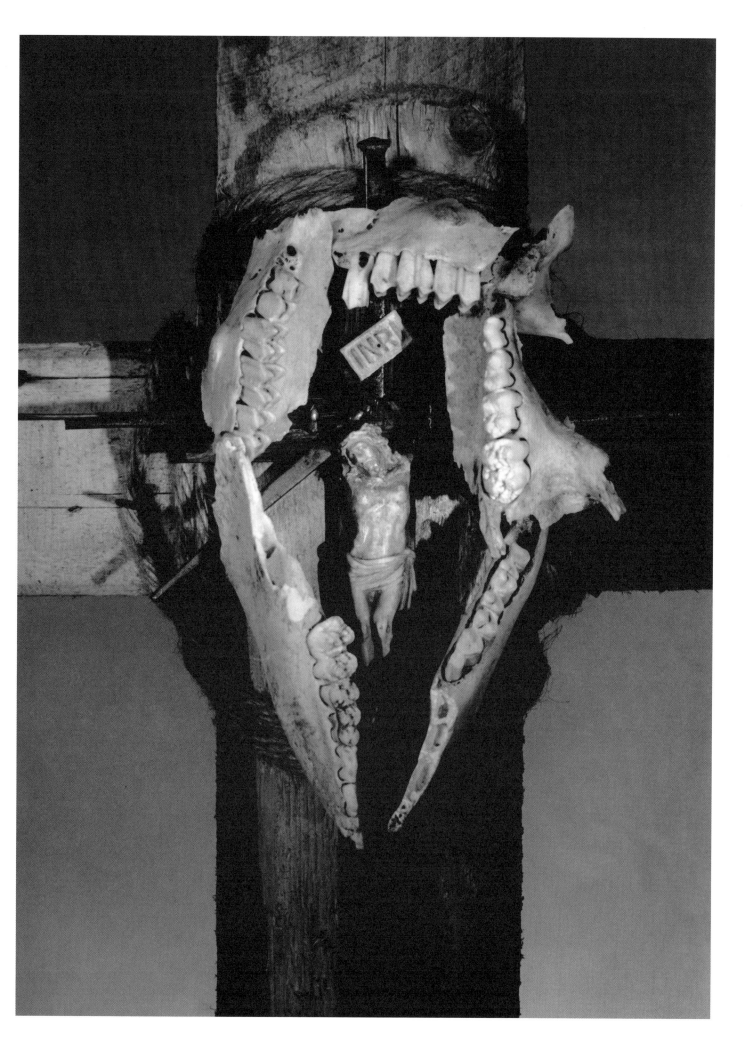

The bleakest and most intensely felt of her war works is also the least specific. Called *Prisoner*, its inspiration came from Rozanne's admiration for the work of Don McCullin, one of Britain's greatest war photographers, whose work of the 1960s and 1970s 'proved so painful and memorable that in 1982 he was forbidden to cover the Falklands War by the British Government of the time.'[7] Hearing him speak on the radio, she was struck by the fact that he too found it difficult to settle into a non-combatant environment, and that, having started to take landscape photographs, he was surprised at the darkness and sombre quality of his images. In its three-dimensionality, *Prisoner* is even more brutal than a photographic depiction of war. Its power rests in the artist's fearless portrayal of a tortured individual, adding proof to the understanding that art 'has the capacity to take us towards a more genuine understanding of the realities of war – particularly difficult to portray in the public domain – and to engage us in a far deeper relationship with its complexities. ...with truths which are necessarily uncomfortable and unsettling by comparison.'[8] It began in 1988 as a male figure, an expression of the fact that wounded soldiers haunt Rozanne. But by the early 1990s it had become a female figure, a shift that allows one to consider not only the women directly affected by war, but those imprisoned in other equally evil ways.

LEFT & ABOVE *Prisoner*, begun in 1988, completed in c.1995, and detail.

At the other extreme are the regimental hearts, which make the point that even very small pieces can be canvases for large statements about war. *He always wanted to be a soldier I and II* were made as a pair in 2006. Their theme is the contrast between the uninformed sentimentality about armed conflict in the past, set against the understanding of its reality today, as a result of unavoidable media coverage. They were inspired by the mainly heart-shaped Victorian and Edwardian regimental pin cushions made as mementos (allegedly made by men for their sweethearts, but more often 'ready-made' with a gap left for the insertion of regimental insignia). Although ultimately shown in the Imperial War Museum's 2008–9 temporary exhibition, *In Memoriam: Remembering the Great War*, the pair were made for no reason other than the need to do so, to assuage her pained vision of a burned body in a tank, a photograph from the first Gulf War still vivid in her mind. Rozanne looked at her own example of an antique pincushion

and asked herself what it would look like today. The result – two pincushions identically boxed – embody innocence and imagined glory on the one hand, and on the other, a reality check in the form of a burnt 'corpse' of bird bones, hanging from a real medal ribbon. To complete the comparison, the first has a trio of bullet casings, the second spent bullets, having been fired. A third, single heart was made especially for her 2009 retrospective. Entitled *Mission Accomplished*, it reflects a combination of the two themes. It is inscribed with names of battlefields and theatres of war, and fittingly, its decorative excesses recall music hall decor. In doing so it can also be said to parody the celebration of war in song, on stage and in film. Rozanne's own life provides a disquieting parallel: her husband Brian played the vicar in the 1977 film, *A Bridge Too Far*, while in 1944 her cousin Rex was at Nijmegen, the penultimate bridge in the real Operation Market-Garden, which aimed to take control of strategic bridges in the Netherlands.

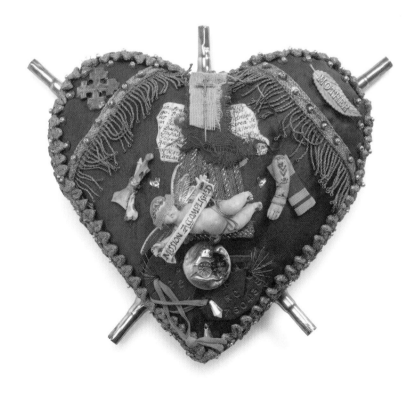

LEFT *Mission Accomplished*, 2008.

ABOVE *He always wanted to be a soldier I and II*, 2006.

The smallest of her images, to be found in *Anthem for Albion*, 2007, also take up the theme of the imagined versus the real, by visualising the journey from eager recruit to hardened soldier, to corpse. It was made as part of the *Mechanical Drawing* project, in which fifteen artists were invited to use Britain's last functioning Schiffli pantograph embroidery machine, at Manchester Metropolitan University. The curators, Melanie Miller and June Hill, explain: 'It was a reading of "The Hewetson Story 1898–1958", Keith Jopp's history of the Macclesfield embroidery company, that provided the spark.'[9] In it, Hewetson's Albion Mill was cited as the place where Schiffli machines stitched 50,000,000 badges for the armies, navies and airforces. Rozanne thought of the women standing hours on end at the machines, and of the men around the world wearing their badges and representing Britain – long ago known as Albion. Her response was a black silk moiré sash decorated with a parade of uniformly stitched badges, individualised by hand painting would-be portraits of young soldiers transfigured by their battles. Reading from right to left, the final badge encloses a double skull wearing the victor's crown of laurels, a representation of both the ultimate sacrifice and the never-ending irony of war. The tension between honour and futility that underpins the imagery in *Anthem* reverberates, *fugato*-like, through all her war-related works, and in this instance was reinforced by the artist's choice of accompanying text: 'Then give Death the crown – For here no Emperor hath won, save He.'[10]

LEFT & ABOVE *Anthem for Albion*, 2007. c.15 painted Schiffli embroidered 'badges' on a silk moiré sash, 195cm long and 15.15cm wide. Photographed as a work in progress by Philip Clarke.

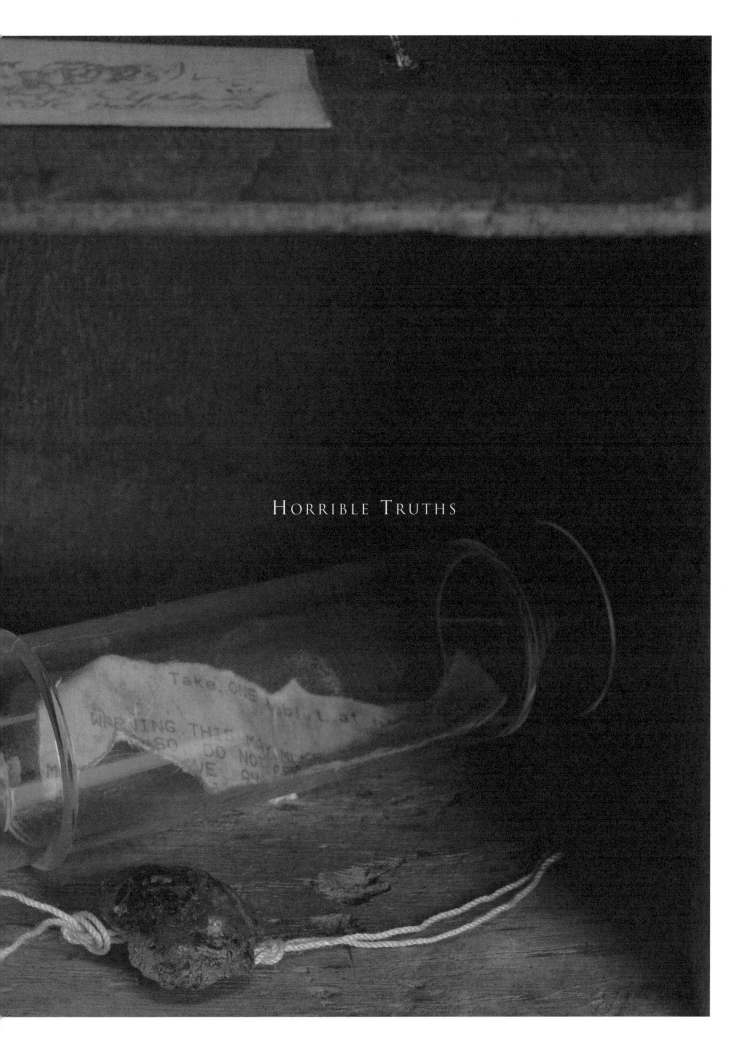

HORRIBLE TRUTHS

It's hard to put a soft spin on a tough life. Surrealism, with its fantastic imagery and incongruous juxtaposition of subject matter, might be the expected route by which Rozanne Hawksley's work strives to express – or expel – the workings of the subconscious, but her process is thoroughly conscious and without a shred of self-pity. These qualities account for her inclusion in *Textile Perspectives in Mixed-Media Sculpture*, whose author, Jac Scott, summed up Rozanne's sculptures as possessing 'a foreboding power that, on close inspection, reveal a slow, painful process of making, meticulous attention to detail, all underpinned with a strong conceptual foundation. The viewer is treated to a visual feast that is enticingly beautiful, yet macabre.'[1] Much of her work articulates her awareness of the social implications of postmodern culture, a fact that accords with her years as an art student, when 'students had never heard of the term "postmodernism", but by the mid-1950s a distinct postmodern sensibility was developing rapidly.'[2] Looking back to her years at art college in Portsmouth and at the RCA, Rozanne when asked about the gallery scene can recall that from Portsmouth she was sent up to London to the Ideal Home Show 'and for some reason walked down Cork St. into a gallery showing Minton, Freud and Bacon, and being absolutely stunned. Then at the Royal, among many others, I remember the Young Contemporaries,' adding with regard to their exhibitions, 'I don't think there was the pressure to sell then.' She herself has remained true to this ethos, only rarely creating work to sell, and then only for a specific commission. Instead, her art is the external manifestation of an inner dialogue. Many of her smaller pieces are intensely personal, while others are extensions of her intimate understanding of the suffering and loss that so often befalls the individual.

While not a feminist, some of her work can be described as gendered, in the sense that it approaches universal themes from a woman's point of view. A study of these can begin with *I will fly south...For Mathew*, a piece begun in 1995, when her son died at the age of 37.[3] The work was, as Rozanne recalls, 'a long time coming together. The piece of wood came in with the tide and was given to me a long time before.' It became the background to a landscape recalling a trip made to Mallorca by Mathew, his girlfriend, Brian and Rozanne, when they knew Mathew's cancer was terminal. 'Mathew and I went to sit in a graveyard and he said, looking up a the mountain with the sun sparkling on its top, "guess what music I'd like for my funeral?", being funny, teasing.' Then, as he died, he said to her 'I know I'm going, it's okay, I shall fly south to the sun and the sea.' The bird rising from the Mallorcan scene has a little sapphire for an eye, a tribute to Mathew's own, 'very blue, always laughing, sparkling,' while the red threads equate to pain and their gradually breaking, to letting him go. Rozanne cannot recall how the piece started, only that she listened to herself and, like many parents in the same position, found within both a loving feeling and anger.

Anger alone motivated a group of four pieces made several years after her husband's death on 28 September 2001. These each in different ways rail at the heavy fist of a kind of Catholicism that kept Brian bound down by his mother and a sense of duty. Indeed, the final piece, *Penitence IV: the book* incorporates one of Brian's own books of penance, its barbed contents bound closed by a weighty chain. While specific to her own reflections on her husband's life and death, *Penitence III: Thou shalt not* has universal meaning as well, being a commentary on the ten commandments, which are also fundamental to Jewish as well as Lutheran, Orthodox, Anglican and other Christian religions. In this case the hypocrisy, the pretence of preaching virtuous character without having it, comes under scrutiny through an allusion to 'Thou shalt not bear false witness'. A rotten wooden and cloth base support a lower jaw and tongue spewing falsehoods that are nevertheless enshrined by the suggestion of a reliquary, in the form of a red seal. Inspired by an old, rotting but beautiful church in Venice, its closest companion, inspired by the same setting, is *Penitence II: the barbed rosary*. Prayer, it implies, may be painful as well as soothing; the penance of incantation may be in its hardship as much as in its demonstration of devotion. Most painful of all is *Penitence I: the garter of penance*. This, as its number implies, was the first of the group, all of which were created in 2006 and 2007. However, its inspiration comes from the ornate yet self-denying practices observed while in Seville in 1989, when she received an Arts Council of Wales travel grant to visit southern Spain. Altogether, *Penitence I–IV* illustrate how impressions gathered years earlier often imbue later work, and at the same time how the making itself can be entirely of and about the moment, for with the completion of the final piece, her anger was dissipated.

LEFT *Penitence III: Thou shalt not*, 2006–07.

TOP *Penitence IV: the book*, 2006–07.

ABOVE *Penitence II: the barbed rosary*, 2006–07.

OVERLEAF *Penitence I: the garter of penance*, 2006–07, detail. A leather garter laced with fish hooks is inscribed with 'make me with spotless mind, pure heart and chaste body…', a prayer to St Joseph.

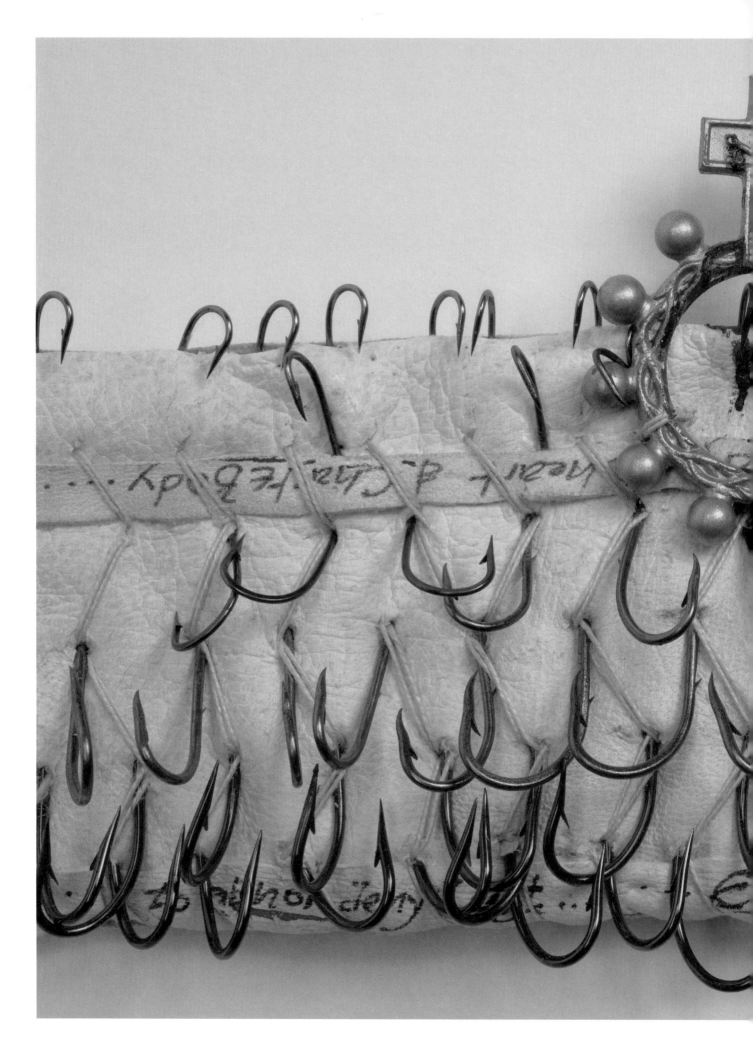

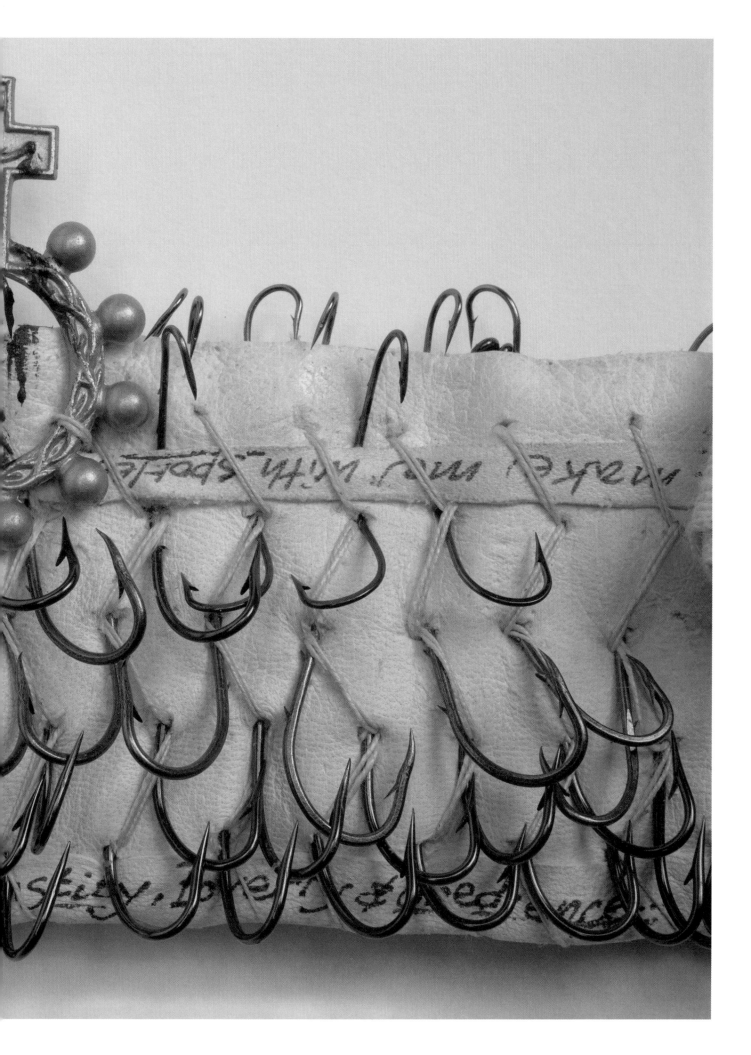

Very different in character is *Goe and catch a falling starre*, a face mask cum fan begun just after Brian died and completed in 2003. Initially undertaken out of a sense of obligation to herself – and to Brian, who just before he died had asked her to go on with her work – it started 'automatically, until I reread the John Donne poem and that reignited the pilot light.' Called *Song,* the poem to which she turned begins thus:

> Go, and catch a falling star,
> Get with child a mandrake root,
> Tell me where all past years are,
> Or who cleft the Devil's foot;
> Teach me to hear Mermaids singing,
> Or to keep off envy's stinging,
> And find
> What wind
> Serves to advance an honest mind.[4]

An ironic poem meaning that a beautiful and faithful wife would be as difficult to find as the falling star, the mandrake-induced pregnancy or a mermaid, it depicts the temptation Donne contends besets all women, that of devilish versus pure love. The same richness of palette and materials spills forward into the second work for Mathew, untitled and completed by about 2005. By then Rozanne's immediate horror at his death had gone, having been replaced by memories of their laughter, and of the fun they had despite hardships, epitomised by the photograph showing her son as a baby, beaming in his second-hand romper suit, given to him by Miss Hornby of the WHI.

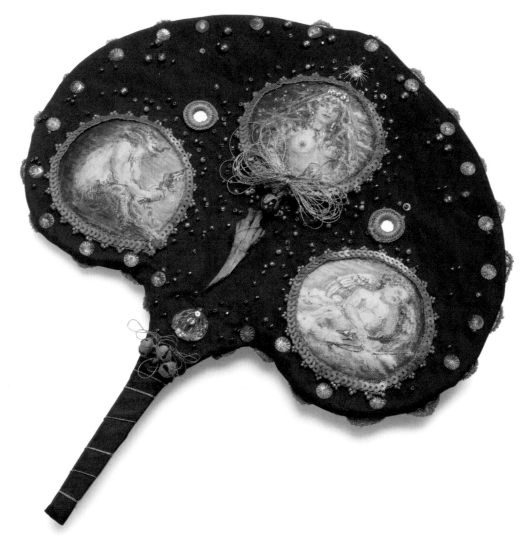

Just as for many women everywhere, pregnancy, birth and death are events that have punctuated Rozanne's life. She conceived five children. Aside from Mathew, two others were miscarried, one aborted, and one, Joanna, survived but a few days. This experience allowed her, with a few words of Spanish, to communicate with a woman in Seville during Holy Week, who wept from joy mingled with weariness at the sight of the Madonna and Child being carried in procession. In 2000 *Nuestra Senora – Madre de Dios* was itself conceived, one of a trio of small Madonnas completed by 2002. Its evident genitalia and sumptuous regalia capture what she understood as much as saw in Seville: 'Our Lady bejewelled; venerated; ever young and pretty; richly adorned under her silver canopy, raised high on men's shoulders – next to me a woman in tears,

poor, worn out with work. She "had a lot of children" she told me. She wept for more than sentiment. ...It's about giving birth, the hidden focus, the almost disposable woman.'[5] Next came the arresting 'alter ego', *Our Lady of the Seven Sorrows*, her purity and calmness holding fast in the face of calamity. Finally, the Madonna entitled *Universal and Eternal*, was begun just before Brian died. Dressed to identify this Madonna with the Balkans, where war had then been waged for a decade, its dark and terrible beauty nevertheless equally enfolds a drama experienced, witnessed and imagined by Rozanne as a child of her times: 'the universal wailing wife and mother of the dead,' who came into being with such clarity that 'she almost made herself.'[6] Of all the works discussed here, this alone has been sold, to close personal friends.

LEFT *Goe and catch a falling starre,* face mask, 2003.

ABOVE *untitled, for Mathew,* c.2005.

OVERLEAF TOP LEFT *Our Lady of the Seven Sorrows* 2000–02. Each Madonna in this series is c.35cm high.

OVERLEAF BELOW LEFT *Nuestra Senora – Madre de Dios,* 2000–02. The first of 'The Three Madonnas' series.

OVERLEAF RIGHT *Universal and Eternal* 2001–02. The last of 'The Three Madonnas' series. Photograph by Philip Clarke.

Most distant from her own experience are the themes behind the two female figures imprisoned in rough wooden cages. Both are works searing in their condemnation of rape as an 'accepted' form of political and military harassment. The first, made in 1990–91, situates the artist's focus of objection by way of its title, *Daughters of Mary, Daughters of Chile*. The red ropes encircling the figure's waist are not merely restraints; red sashes, as also seen in *Nuestra Senora*, are worn by pregnant women in traditional Spanish-speaking cultures to prevent the child from being deformed, here clearly an ineffectual measure. The power of its sequel of 1992, *Virgin with child*, is in the rendering of the rape victim's deep humiliation, whose moving presence is all the more remarkable given her diminutive size, which is only some 50 centimetres (20 inches) high. Although the second work is more universal in its reflections, both derive from the media focus on the lack of women's rights in Chile that became apparent after the Chilean elections of 1989 and its subsequent transition to democracy.[7] Both were also initiated during the period when Rozanne was a visiting tutor and external examiner at the RCA

and Goldsmiths. The latter had revised its diploma course into an MA, first awarded in 1992 under the leadership of Janis Jefferies. Jefferies recalls Rozanne's contribution during her three years as examiner, from 1991–94, as 'bringing the experience of the practitioner who was committed to socially engaged practice – issue based, incredibly sculptural.'[8]

OPPOSITE *Virgin with child*, 1992, 65cm high. Exhibited in that year at the National Eisteddfod of Wales, Aberystwyth.

LEFT *Daughters of Mary, Daughters of Chile*, 1990–91.

ABOVE *Virgin with child*, 1992, detail.

It is easy to overlook the impact of a teacher whose entire body of work has never been seen or documented, and in addition, whose consistent inclusion in exhibitions began in 1991, when she was sixty. Today, her work accords with much that finds its way into *avant garde* galleries and publications, yet there was a time when it did not. But one indication of this was *Decorations*, a piece Rozanne exhibited at the RIBA in 1986 (related to *We are legion* and no longer extant). Carole Murphy, unknown to Rozanne until Carole introduced herself recently by letter, saw it and has 'never forgotten it; looking back, I realise how truly impactful it was – and courageous – in the context of the other work displayed.'[9] Rozanne's unique stance is confirmed by Audrey Walker: 'What did she bring to her teaching? Of course, her knowledge of many arts – theatre, music, poetry, painting – and especially the world of textiles and fashion and the skills needed to manipulate cloth. But above all it was her conviction that students needed to think, feel, draw and focus on the inner essentials of their ideas, and to have the commitment and courage to carry them through. "Courage" and "No Compromises" are the marks of her own work. Over the years she has exploded any pre-conceived notions of what a "textile work" can be, in either form or subject matter. The work can be sumptuous or spare, tiny or room-size, and layered with symbolic references. It exists in that perilous area where categorisation is impossible and, as such, it continues to challenge us all.'[10] That Rozanne defies classification stems

from her response to media. She says, 'I work with those materials and those only that are necessary to my emotional thought process... with those that impel me to select them, whatever they may be.' To this she adds, 'very often I have little or no knowledge of the working of non-textile components – exciting but frustrating in that it can take so long to achieve my aim.'

Noticeable, too, is Rozanne's fascination with death. Yet even the rendering of herself overlaid with Brian's form, drawn when he died, is tender, without a trace of gruesome, grisly morbidity. Jane Wildgoose recounts an episode that clarifies this point: 'I first met Rozanne around 1980 when, as a recent graduate, I was working as technician in Printed Textiles in the Embroidery Department at Goldsmiths College in London. Roz was studying on the postgraduate course and she came into the print room with a book about William Morris to ask if it would be possible for her to reproduce one of the designs in it on cloth. I distinctly remember thinking that this was not a particularly inspiring proposition, but I did assure her that it could be done. Roz was obviously pleased, and explained that she wanted to replace all the flowers in the design with skulls and urns, and to print the whole thing in black, on a black background. At this I let out a kind of yelp of enthusiasm, and we began an excitable conversation in which we discovered that we shared a lively interest in Victorian mourning customs and costume'.

'At that time there was little published on the subject, and it was rare to meet

RIGHT *Self-portrait,* of Rozanne remembering Brian after his death, late 2001.

anyone who considered the funereal customs of the past to be anything more than an eccentric and rather morbid irrelevance. Nowadays, though, if you type "death, mourning, Victorian" into Google, a long list appears: there are publications, exhibitions, and discussions, from academics, artists and designers. Roz was years ahead of her time, and in consequence, her work did not always sit comfortably with that of the rest of her generation. Today, however, it is as though the world has gradually caught up with her.'[11]

Among the funereal customs Rozanne recalls fondly are those of her Great Auntie Lizzie, whose husband, Tom Downton, looked after the church graveyard in Radipole.[12] Visiting every summer from a very young age until Auntie died while Rozanne was at the RCA, she remembers the 'beautifully handmade broderie anglais nightgown (including Dorset buttons), she made out of her own hand-sewn trousseau, fine knitted stockings and a bonnet with soft real lace. Of course, Auntie kept it clean, and it was on a bed, all laid out, in a room entirely filled by that bed.'

Such memories she has carried forward in an intermingling of the great times and the grey times. She tells another story of the girl living behind the Unique Cleaners in one room, pregnant by a handsome young man, fainting in the egg basket in Sainsbury's in Kensington High Street. It hardly matters whether it is her or a fiction – or another gal from the RCA. It was an era when difficult pregnancies and the death of children were commonplace and borne in silence, or at the very least, in some faraway corner of the country. Rozanne speaks in a kind of shorthand about such traditions: 'went to a farm in Kent, did murals on walls of an oast-house, went also for interviews as mother's help; picking brussels sprouts and fell down the bank, child born in bits, all so kind...'. Typically, she instantly turns to a happy tale of her host family's relative, landed gentry from Dorset, who had known Uncle Tom's father. 'Are you sure?', she asked, and the pleasing reply was 'Yes, in the harvest festivals Tom's father in his smock would sing the diary of the year.' It was

never so easy to lay to rest the ghost of little Joanna Scott, Rozanne's severely deformed thalidomide baby whose appearance drove her first husband into a raving grief, and whose common grave she found with Brian and Mathew in 1990. For Joanna, Rozanne did finally make *Bye Bye Baby: take one every morning*, in 2008. Its single angry fist shakes emblematically at the pharmaceutical companies who had evidence from late 1956 that their pill for morning sickness caused thousands of babies to be stillborn or deformed; Joanna was among the last, born in May 1961, only some ten months before the drug was withdrawn. This, an unnatural death, justifies the blunt imagery, the similitude to a cabinet of curiosities. In contrast is the gentle and loving depiction of *Orpheus* (see Chapter Three), which was made for Brian, aged 80 when he died. His life was full and, as Orphean legend contends, his song will go on. For Rozanne, that song began with an acrostic love poem to her, penned by Brian and beginning with the words, 'Read my mind aloud...'.

LEFT *Bye Bye Baby: take one every morning*, 2008.
ABOVE Acrostic poem written about Rozanne by Brian, New Year's Eve, 1970 and which he gave to her on New Year's Day 1971.

A KIND OF PEACE

Although Rozanne Hawksley's materials range from cloth, jewels and thread to wood, clay and bones, it remains possible to study her approach to the physicality of her work by looking in depth at one medium: the glove. These have been at times the means and, at others, an end in itself. She has collected them, like – and she laughs at herself – 'a woman taking in stray cats, or lost waifs.' In London with Brian, one or the other would cry 'Oh look! There's one...' and it would be rescued. It would be a mistake, however, to see this as mere sentimentality. Rather, it is a kind of anthropology, 'which tries to engage with the minutiae of everyday life while retaining a commitment to understanding humanity as a whole.'[1] For Rozanne, gloves represent those who have used them or made them, as well as the possibility of profound attachment to them and sadness at their loss. Those that are white stand for peace, and for the Royal Marines she loved to watch as a girl. In addition, they are a constant in her work, from the 1950s – when they were required wear for smart young women and, in her first job at Guildford, when she taught the design and making of gloves and belts – to their use in the seminal works of 1987 and 1991 (both sharing in their title the words, *Pale Armistice*) and beyond to the present day. Among her smaller works, those being gloves or composed of gloves are also the most exhibited, giving rise to a body of commentary that allows for an assessment of her place in the continuum of postmodernist and neo-mannerist art.

There is no doubt about the impact of *Pale Armistice*. It began life in 1984, when Rozanne read about St Mary's Church and The Virgins' Crowns and Gloves, in Abbotts Ann, Hampshire. This church retains the medieval custom that allows those who have died unmarried and of unblemished reputation the right to a 'crown', carried in procession and then hung near the ceiling of the church. Traditionally, these included personal items such as gloves, of kid or of paper.[2] Rozanne imagined such a wreath, but for a woman wrongly supposed to be a virgin, so its gloves were very rough and bloodied. Never quite satisfied with this wreath, called *Wreath for a virgin*, its symbolism remained potent and by 1986–87 the first *Pale Armistice* was underway, 'made in the wake of the Falklands campaign [and] a wry comment on its victories.' This version was selected by Pennina Barnett for *The Subversive Stitch*, an exhibition whose two related parts included one looking at 'Women and Textiles Today', shown at Manchester's Cornerhouse in 1988. Placing it with other objects responding to the topic of peace and protest in Britain, Barnett highlighted the fact that its gloves were 'no longer pristine but marked and worn, they join together in grief, comfort and healing.'[3]

PREVIOUS *Pale Armistice*, made for the Imperial War Museum, 1991, detail. Photograph by Damon Cleary, courtesy of the Imperial War Museum.

LEFT *Pale Armistice: in death only are we united*, 1987. Shown in *The Subversive Stitch* exhibition at the Cornerhouse, Manchester, in 1988. Photographed by Brian Hawksley. In the collection of the Embroiderers' Guild.

RIGHT Cover of *Legion* October/November 1998, its issue in remembrance of the 80th anniversary of the end of World War I, showing *Pale Armistice*.

Rozanne herself wrote of the work in 1987, giving it its full title – *Pale Armistice: in death only are we united* – and noting that she had already worked 'for a number of years using the glove as a symbol of the human individual and in this piece, each one is representative of one who has fought some kind of battle, public or private; as an enforced combatant (with an awful kind of innocence) or a relative or friend of that fighter, caught up in the battle.' To this she added, 'This state of war seems un-ending and only in death are we united in an enviable peace.'[4] Although the exhibition had objects resulting from open submission, Rozanne's piece was pre-selected. In retrospect it has become closely associated with the show – equally as connected to its radical commitment to extending the debate surrounding women, textiles and femininity, as to its attention to 'the covert ways embroidery has provided a source of support and satisfaction for women.'[5] For many, 'Rozanne Hawksley <u>was</u> *The Subversive Stitch*.'[6]

With that wreath purchased for the Embroiderers' Guild Collection, Rozanne made another version at the request of the Imperial War Museum. This new wreath, known only by the short title, *Pale Armistice*, was completed in 1991. Almost immediately, it was on show elsewhere, in *Declarations of War: Contemporary Art from the Collection of the Imperial War Museum*, an exhibition open at Kettle's Yard Gallery, Cambridge, during the first two months of 1993. John McEwen of the *Sunday Telegraph* singled it out as a 'memorable object', noting that, 'Apart from its striking originality as

a *memento mori* it has undeniable pathos, summed up in the visitors' book by Flora Stewart, aged six: "The white wreath made me think death is a very sad thing." It is indeed, and sometimes we rationalise the sadness out of it too much.'[7] In *The Independent*, where it was illustrated alongside works by Epstein, Millais and Pollock, James Hall described it as 'haunting because of the mixed feelings it inspires towards the dead. Individually, these limp and ghostly hands are pitiful, but taken *en masse*, they are cloying. Their fingers seem to cling to the present like white fungus.'[8] The wreath is also the only image related to this exhibition to be found in the Gallery's spring 1993 leaflet, and its growing fame since then can be attributed, in part, to its photogenic nature. During the commemorations of the 80th anniversary of the end of the First World War, for example, it appeared on two covers, one the IWM *What's On* leaflet for September 1998 to January 1999 and the other, the October/November 1998 issue of *Legion*, the magazine of the Royal British Legion. Having achieved something of a 'mascot' status, it has been on IWM literature continuously since 2000.[9]

What makes *Pale Armistice* so compelling is the fusion of 'the poetic idea and its pictorial statement,' something written about Adrian Ryan's work but appropriate to Rozanne's as well, not least because he too worked with a single widely recognised form, in his case, fish. In 1994 Ryan – best man at her first wedding, lecturing in painting and drawing at

Goldsmiths during most of Rozanne's years there, and 'Uncle Jim' to Mathew – explained why he painted fish: no two are identical 'and each has its own character, as shown by the placing of two or more together. It is the poetry inherent in their uniqueness and agelessness that the artist hopes to portray... [capturing] the face of his own fate, from which he learns that death too has a beauty of its own.'[10] He might well be writing of gloves instead. Rozanne's repetition of gloves, their arrangement so as to highlight their 'themes and variations', not only brings her *fugato* approach to the fore, but also makes each inseparable from the other. The gloves become like hands held, or clasped, or shaken, all together indicating human connections, whether in fun, fondness or formality. This humanitarian lyricism is in stark contrast to the disturbing isolationist effect of a lone glove caught on a length of barbed wire in *After Łódź* (or *Glove on a wire II*), a late 1980s installation that attempted to rethink a journey towards the unknown, in this case the concentration camp outside Łódź for Jews, Gypsies, Catholics and homosexuals, all labelled 'undesirables' under the Nazi regime. The same sense of solitude or segregation can be found in the very recent work, *Łódź re-visited*, as well as in *Stigmata*. Exhibited in *Death*, the Kettle's Yard 1988 exhibition, *Stigmata* then had a more complex boxed background,[11] now reduced to the stigmatised baby's glove surrounded by jet beads. It symbolises the power of authoritarianism over the young, the massacre of innocents – and of innocence – and the pain of confinement or incarceration.

TOP *Stigmata*, 1988, 18cm high.

ABOVE *Łódź re-visited*, 2008–09, 30cm high. The portcullis-like wooden frame was given to Rozanne some thirty years before and itself dates from before the First World War. Photograph by Philip Clarke.

Rozanne's long-standing interest in gloves can be traced back to the hands of her seamstress grandmother, who used them as cover for pin-pricked fingers. She recalls being fascinated when taken along to Handley's in Southsea, where her mother purchased gloves, and equally in awe of the contents of a leather shop in London's Foubert Place (crossing Carnaby Street), where, in search of leather for her students at Guildford decades later, she was shown 'beautiful gloving leather – they had leather that was like silk, dyed with a sable brush no wider than an inch so none of the colour passed inside.' She absorbed the protocol surrounding gloves given as gifts at funerals: white for the rich mourners and more practical black for the workers. Most of all, however, as a child she loved the ritual of trying the gloves on: 'there would be this incredible violet velvet-covered support to rest the arm against, almost coffin-like, and when I sold inexpensive millinery at Jay's they still had them there too.' Something of these traditions spill forward into *Continuum*, a work begun prior to 1987 and having several forms since then. It was shown at Camden Art Centre, London and, in 1993, was included in an exhibition of sculptures at Margam Park, Port Talbot, Wales. The long line of nailed gloves denoted torture going on and on; the last was a plain piece of glove with a pile of nails at the ready. Over a decade later, the urge to depict lost lives in this way arose again, resulting in a 'reredos' of thirteen gloves, entitled *In whose name*. In this work, completed in 2002, a larger central plank holds a form-filled, lace-gauntleted glove. As a symbol of life after death, its positioning on a cross and with a rosary reinforces its distinction from the other gloves (one of which is shown here, in detail).

LEFT *In whose name,* 2000–02, begun in 2000, completed in 2002. One of Brian Hawksley's last photographs.

TOP Single nailed glove from the lower left section of *In whose name*, 2002.

ABOVE *Continuum*, 1987. Photograph by Brian Hawksley.

A very different kind of torture – that of the deceived and unloved woman – is the subject of a 2006 work, *Get thee to a nunnery*. Encased in a manner inspired by the wall cases in the museum in Nafhlion, Greece, as if to underscore the antiquity of its meaning, it portrays the taunt of Hamlet to Ophelia: 'why wouldst thou be a breeder of sinners?'

In far more magisterial vein are the elaborate, single gloves, inspired by the sight of late Tudor and early Stuart examples held in the collection of the Museum of Costume, Bath. The first of these is *Et ne non inducas (And lead us not)*, completed in 1989. Three years later came *Libera me, Domine, de morte aeterna (Deliver me, oh Lord, from eternal death)*. Although written of the first, both could be described as conceived 'entirely in the spirit of Jacobean or early Baroque jewels...[combining] richness and exquisite detailing with the kind of programmatic meaning so beloved by seventeenth-century makers and their cultivated patrons.'[12] Similarly, descriptions of the second glove

TOP *Get thee to a nunnery,* 2006. The box in profile is deeper at the top than at the bottom, to suggest museum wall cases such as those seen in the Nafplion Folk Art Museum, during a trip to Greece made in 2002.

ABOVE *Et ne non inducas (And lead us not)*, begun in 1987 and completed in 1989, 22cm long. Exhibited in 2005, together with *One has to be so careful these days*, at SOFA, Chicago, and in 2006 in *Aspects of Narrative in Contemporary Textiles in Wales*, at Ruthin Craft Centre.

RIGHT *Pale Rider,* 2008, detail. Inspired by the Revelation to St John, the last canonical book of the New Testament in the Christian Bible.

as 'a sombre confection' and 'stunning yet slightly macabre' would do equally well for the first.[13] This is because both reflect the vanitas style of painting particularly associated with the Spanish Netherlands in the earlier part of the seventeenth century. Such symbolic still life paintings often included skulls and were reminders of the transience of life, details that make *Pale Rider*, a work of 2008, the third and latest of this group. It contains the most direct warnings against the celebration of trivial pleasures, with its title a reference to the Fourth Horseman of the Apocalypse, named as Death, and its seal-ring with a Roman IV referring to the fourth seal in the Revelation to St John: 'the heavens shall be dissolved, and the air shall be thrown into utter confusion.' All seven seals of Revelation find parallels in the seven strewn bones, which catalogue the dangers of a world focused on privilege and power. In a final twist of irony, the very form Rozanne has chosen – the exquisite and aristocratic glove – was often worn by Cavaliers (those supporting

King Charles I) and the term, from the Spanish *caballarius*, meaning horseman, already meant an overbearing swashbuckler or swaggering gallant by the early 1600s.

The sense of 'series' in these gloved works is both real and accidental. In reality, what they share is the artist's visual vocabulary, enriched as it is by immersion in written works, travel and contemporary events. The accidental aspect occurs because the choice of similar materials or form is never made deliberately, but only because the piece demands it. In some cases it is the need to incorporate something given to her by a friend that prompts Rozanne's choices. This was the case with *For Brian: our revels now are ended* (2006–07), which incorporates a found cotton glove with shards from Brian's *Hamlet* and, at the cuff and around the inner edge of the box, black ribbon given to her by Eirian Short. It is also true for *In whose name*, in which the lace was from pieces among a large collection that was a gift from another embroidering textile artist, Diana Springall.

ABOVE *Libera me, domine, de morte aeterna (Deliver me, oh Lord, from eternal death)*, 1992. The jewelled skull represents life on this earth, and the three pearls (like the three lilies in Pale Armistice) symbolise the Trinity.

RIGHT *For Brian: our revels now are ended*, 2006–07, detail. The ribbon on the cuff, which also surrounds the inner edge of the glove's box, is stitched with words and phrases in memory of Brian.

'Sometimes it's important to have something of the real person', she says, turning to *Aimez-vous le big Mac?*, a memorial glove finished in 2008. Its silk chiffon and gold-thread laden black fabric were being worked into a dress by the deceased, whose love of nature and the outdoors is signified by the gauntlet lining of blue silk. Birth stones match in number the years of his life and the thimble and needles denote his embroidery skills, while the wand alludes to his work for an opera house in Paris, where he died. This, a genuine *memento mori*, has an animation suggestive of a real character, more evident when juxtaposed to *Queen of Spades*, made during the same period but taking its inspiration from fiction (see Chapter Five). These are not small differences, but fundamental to the artist's approach, which devotes long periods of time to 'the decision of "how?" and "with what?" which leads to the use of only those materials and no others, that are absolutely necessary to the thinking.' As if to stress how demanding these periods of selection can be, to this she adds, 'All work is a risk.'[14]

LEFT *Aimez-vous le big Mac?*, 2008, detail. Exhibited in *Stuff: contemporary textiles by The 62 Group* at the Catmose Gallery, Leicestershire, Spring 2008.

ABOVE *Queen of Spades*, 2008. Inspired by the story of the same name by Pushkin.

Metamorphosis is an amalgam of the found and the hoarded. Rozanne explains: 'This piece came to life in 2006 after a visit four years earlier with Audrey Walker to a quiet valley in the Peloponnese, on the slope of which was a tiny domed Orthodox church. Brian had recently died and I was of course missing him and, as always, Mathew. I sensed here a kind of peace and spent some time alone, letting my mind rest, I suppose. I knew a kind of finality, that a passing (NOT an ending) had occurred as I walked out into the sun, and I picked up a piece of broken tile and some olive leaves at the side of the track.' It seems telling that the hand here is a doll's hand, with a tangible 'otherness' and lack of frailty, so different from the baby's glove in a work of 1982–83, entitled *Sine Nomine (without name)*. This was the first *memento mori* for baby Joanna and is composed entirely of things thrown away: a cross from a cemetery, a lost glove, dead leaves from a discarded wreath, and a bird, pushed from its nest and once feathered, but a skeleton now. Of this work, as for all others, Rozanne speaks of knowing only 'the initial feel or essence of mind and material. I offer up continuously and the piece grows towards an often unforeseen conclusion.' Of this process, June Hill, curator of Rozanne's 2009 retrospective, urges us to 'note the words

and of what they speak: openness; a sense of listening and looking; responsiveness to something that is felt but not always known; a process of discernment; an authenticity of materials and of making. And a letting go, an offering up: a loss of self at the very moment that the self is expressed.' This perceptive analysis continues: 'Rozanne Hawksley's work addresses the most visceral experiences of life: love and loss; suffering and war; isolation, poverty, power and its abuse. Her range is immense: each piece taking the form it appears to demand. The ideas are intensely felt and intensely executed. References are explicit and implicit. They combine that which is revealed and that which is withheld. Materials and images are intuitively selected for their innate sense of rightness; for that of which they speak – an empty glove, a lily, the drape of sheer chiffon cut on the bias, bleached bones, a photograph. These are deeply evocative works. They are individual expressions of contingent realities. They are as tangible recollections of that which has been experienced, and of that which continues to be felt. For those who have endured the tenderings of life, the empathy with these works is all too real. They have said: "Thank you for expressing that of which we cannot speak ourselves".' [15]

ABOVE *Metamorphosis*, 2006, approximately 12cm across. The fragment of tile and olive branches were collected in Greece in 2002.

RIGHT *Sine Nomine (without name)*, 1982–83, detail. The first *memento mori* for Rozanne's daughter Joanna, composed entirely of materials that had been discarded.

This drama inherent in Rozanne's work is essential to her being, as much engraved in her own mind as it is transcribed into her work. Thus perhaps the final words belong to Alan Bennett, whose first London West End play, *Forty Years On*, is another text often revisited by Rozanne, partly because for ten days Brian had replaced John Gielgud in it and 'had woo'd me by leaning up against the wall in my little room in Roehampton and quoting from it – he loved Bennett's work' – and partly because it has become increasingly meaningful in Rozanne's artistic practice. For example, it contributed to the 2007 work *Caiaphas*, a wreath for mourning the death of nature named for one who, according to William Blake, mistakenly thought he was a benefactor of mankind.[16] An extract from Bennett's text, first performed in 1968, is also incorporated in one of Rozanne's most recent pieces, *In the Beginning...*, which looks back to the thoughtless progress of the 'now, the world of the lay-by and the civic improvement scheme' but speaks, too, of tomorrow, just as does the Headmaster in Act 2 of Bennett's *Forty Years On:*[17] 'Country is park and shore is marina, spare time is leisure and more, year by year. We have become a battery people, a people of under-privileged hearts fed on pap in darkness, bred out of all taste and season to savour the shoddy splendours of the new civility. The hedges come down from the silent fields. The lease is out on the corner site. A butterfly is an event.' Conveyed in the play with wry irreverence this passage is followed here by another from Act 1, of central relevance to a more serene Rozanne, who finds in it that endearing and enduring characteristic of humanity, hope:

'...and then as the light seeped back into the sky; suddenly, just before dawn, we heard the nightingales.'

LEFT *Maiden's Garland,* 2009.

ABOVE *Caiaphas,* 2007. Juxtaposing delicate bones and jewels to underscore the beauty of nature in all its forms.

OVERLEAF *Caiaphas,* 2007, detail.

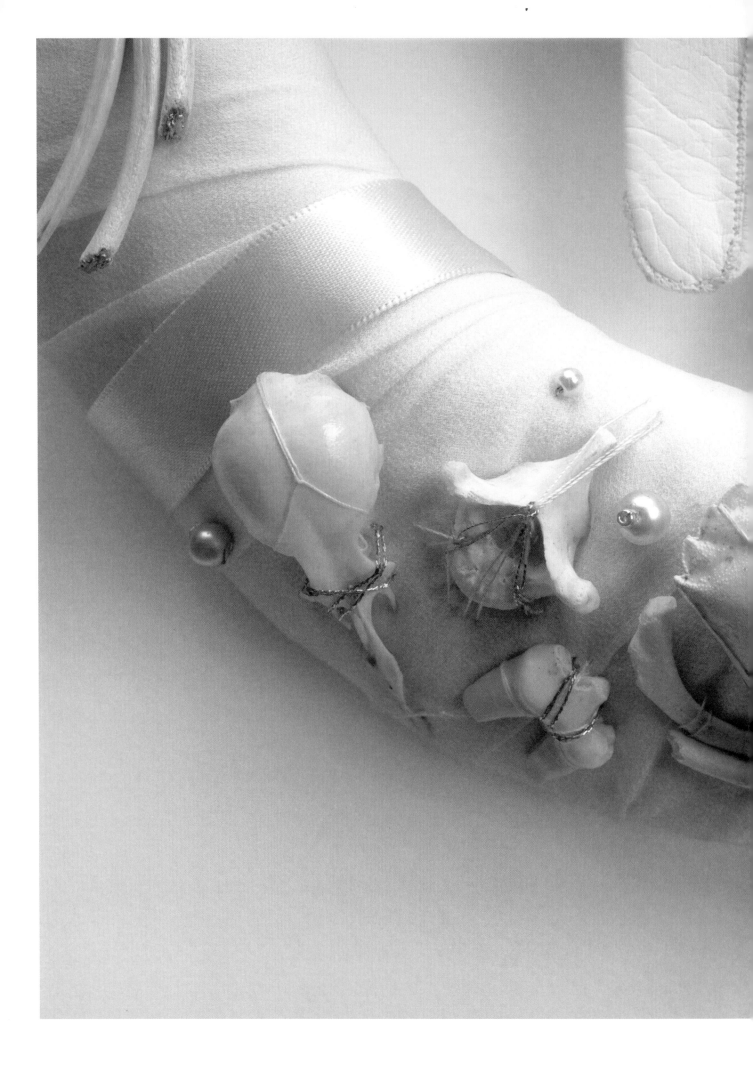

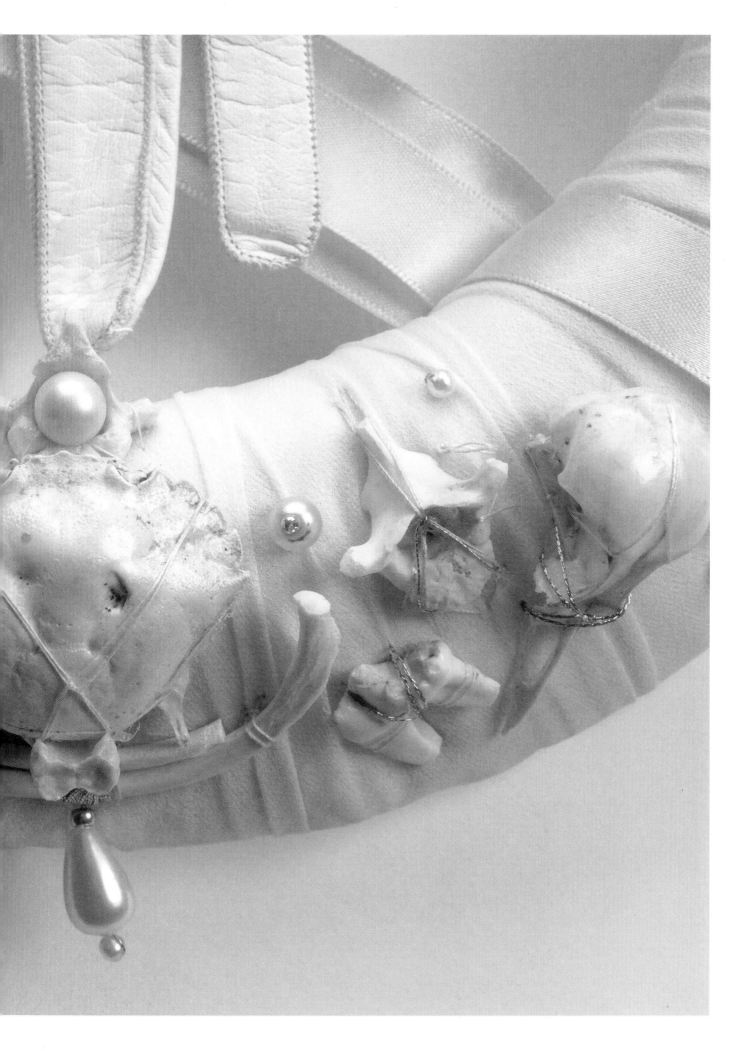

BIOGRAPHY

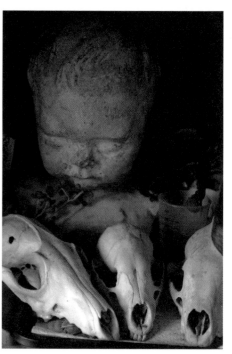

Rozanne's working environment, 2008.

ROZANNE HAWKSLEY (nee Pibworth)
Born 18 February 1931

EDUCATION

Southern College of Art, Portsmouth, NDD, 1951

Royal College of Art (Fashion School), ARCA, 1954

Goldsmiths College, Advanced (Postgraduate) Diploma, 1980

CAREER

1954–63 Freelance designer/maker (including work for the WHI), illustrator and columnist, part-time tutor at Brighton and Guildford colleges of art

1964–67 Designing, teaching and lecturing at the American Needlework Center, Washington DC

1967–68 Designing and teaching at the WHI, London, and Brighton and Portsmouth colleges of art

1968–78 Lecturer and, from 1969, Senior Lecturer, Battersea College of Education

1980–87 Part-time tutor Goldsmiths College (Textiles); visiting tutor Royal College of Art and Slade School of Fine Art, London

1991–93 Visiting tutor and external examiner to the Royal College of Art and Goldsmiths College, London

1987 Established current studio in Pembrokeshire, Wales

SOLO EXHIBITIONS

2009 *Rozanne Hawksley: Offerings*
Ruthin Craft Centre (and touring)

2009 *In the Beginning: Offerings Reducere*
Knitting & Stitching Show, London, Dublin and Harrogate

2007 *The Seamstress and the Sea*
Portsmouth City Museum

2006–07 *The Seamstress and The Sea*
HMS Belfast/Imperial War Museum

2000 '*...a treaty will be signed some time today*'
Knitting & Stitching Show, London, Dublin and Harrogate

1998 *Rozanne Hawksley*
Sessions Gallery Newport, Wales

1997 '*...a treaty will be signed some time today*'
Mission Gallery, Swansea

1995 *The Colour Orange*
Myles Meehan Gallery, Darlington

GROUP SHOWS

2008–09 *In Memoriam: Remembering...*
Imperial War Museum, London

2008 *Stuff:...62 Group*
The Catmose Gallery, Leicestershire

2007–08 *Mechanical Drawing: the schiffli project*
The Holden Gallery, MMU Manchester;
The Hub, Sleaford; Farfield Mill,
Sedbergh; Macclesfield Silk Museum;
Knitting & Stitching Show,
Birmingham, London and Harrogate

2007 *Flossie and Me*
Imperial War Museum, London

2006 *Gweld Llais a Chlywed Llun
– Aspects of Narrative in Contemporary
Art Textiles in Wales*
The Gallery, Ruthin Craft Centre

2006 *Witness-Highlights*
Imperial War Museum, North,
Manchester

2006 *Tracing Threads*
Hove Museum and Art Gallery

2005 *SOFA, Chicago*
The Gallery, Ruthin Craft Centre

2005 *Ceremony*
Pump House Gallery, London

2004 *Of Sea and Stars*
Mission Gallery, Swansea

2004 *Of Material Concern*
Millennium Galleries, Sheffield

2003 *Sample at Art of the STITCH*
Williamson Galleries, Birkenhead
Tilburg Textile Museum, Holland

2003 *Gweld Llais a Chlywed Llun
– Aspects of Narrative in Contemporary
Art Textiles in Wales*
National Eisteddfod of Wales, Meifod

2003 *Material Spaces*
Tullie House, Carlisle

2002 *Visual Arts and Crafts Exhibition*
National Eisteddfod of Wales, St David's

2001 *Network*
Bishop's Palace, St David's, Pembrokeshire

2000 *Endings*
Whitworth Gallery, Manchester

1999 *10 x 10 (in support of Mencap)*
Knitting & Stitching Show, London,
Dublin and Harrogate

1998 *The First World War Remembered*
Imperial War Museum

1998 *On the Edge*
Knitting & Stitching Show, Tatton
Park Cheshire, London, Dublin
and Harrogate

1994–95 *Box*
Walsall Museum and Art Gallery

1993 *Sculpture at Margam*
Margam Park, Port Talbot

1993 *Declarations of War*
Kettle's Yard Gallery, Cambridge

1993 *No More Heroes Anymore*
The Royal Scottish Academy, Edinburgh

1992 *Visual Arts and Crafts Exhibition*
National Eisteddfod of Wales,
Aberystwyth

1992 *Out of the Frame*
Crafts Council, London; Mercer Art
Gallery, Harrogate; Herbert Art Gallery
and Museum, Coventry; Aberystwyth
Art Centre; Plymouth City Art Gallery;
Peter Scott Gallery, Lancaster University

1992 *International Triennial*
Central Museum of Textiles,
Łódź, Poland

1991 *Network*
Bishop's Palace, St David's, Pembrokeshire

1988 *Subversive Stitch*
Cornerhouse, Manchester

1988 *Death*
Kettles Yard Gallery, Cambridge

1986 *Stitched Textiles for Interiors*
Royal Institute of British Architects,
London

1985 *62 Group Show*
Museum of Modern Art, Tokyo;
touring to Kyoto and Osaka, Japan

1980–81 *Embroiderers' Guild Exhibition*
Commonwealth Institute, London

AWARDS

2006 Arts Council of Wales Exhibition
Award, for *The Seamstress and the Sea*

1992 British Council Travel Award,
for travel to Poland

1989 Arts Council of Wales Study Grant,
for travel to Southern Spain

COLLECTIONS AND COMMISSIONS

Embroiderers' Guild, London

Imperial War Museum, London

Łódź Central Museum of Textiles, Poland

Andrew Salmon, Creative Exhibitions

Whitelands College, University of Surrey,
Roehampton

Worshipful Company of Weavers for the
Bishop of London

Rozanne's working environment, 2008.

Notes & Further Reading

The Seamstress and the Sea

1   Unless otherwise stated, all quotations are from Rozanne Hawksley, *The Seamstress and the Sea*, exhibition information sheet (London: Imperial War Museum), October 2006, and from taped interviews with the artist, January–July 2008.

2   *Art of the STITCH and SAMPLE* (London: Embroiderers' Guild), 2003, p.49.

3   *Ibid*, p.50.

Where's Wilfred?

1   See, for example, the BBC School Radio, World War II Audio Clips Library: http://www.bbc.co.uk/schoolradio/history/worldwar2 audioclipslibrary.shtml within which is clip no.3, 'Children being evacuated from London on 1/9/1939'.

2   John Hunter, 'Words of Wisdom, Generally Speaking', *The Sunday Mirror*, June 11, 2000, accessed on http://findarticles.com July 29, 2008.

3   A broadcast of interviews by Lyn MacDonald, which formed a prelude to her publication, *They Called It Passchendaele: Story of the Third Battle of Ypres and of the Men Who Fought in It* (London: Michael Joseph Ltd), October 1979.

4   Ned Temko and Mark Townsend, *The Observer*, Sunday November 11, 2007: http://www.guardian.co.uk/uk/2007/nov/11/iraq.iraq

5   The poem can be read at www.gutenberg.org/etext/1321

6   See also Mary Schoeser, *More is More: an antidote to minimalism* (London: Conran Octopus), 2002, p.155.

7   Matthew 4.1: 'Then was Jesus led up of the Spirit into the wilderness to be tempted by the devil.' King James Version. See also Judith Peacock, 'The Poor Relation: Ecclesiastical Embroidery', *Embroidery*, Vol.54, No.4, July 2003, pp.36–39, available at http://embroidery.embroiderersguild.com/20034/peacock.htm

8   See, for example, Albert Barnes, *Notes, Critical, Illustrative & Practical on the Book of Job: With a New Translation & an Introductory Dissertation* (New York: Leavitt & Allen) 1854, p.278; digitized 17 February, 2006 from an original from the University of Michigan: http://books.google.com/books?id=fscCVhGZMC8C&dq

9   Rozanne Pibworth-Hawksley, 'Marks of Significance: a mitre for the Bishop of London', *The World of Embroidery*, Vol.50, No.2, March 1999, pp.91–2.

10 Rian Evans, 'Fabrication: Creative grit generates a tactile response to life and death issues – Picking the bones out of textiles', *The Western Mail*, a Wednesday in September, November or December 1998, p.12; from Rozanne's collection of press cuttings.

Man about Town

1   Samuel Smiles and Peter W. Sinnema (ed.), *Self Help* revised editions (New York: Oxford University Press), 2002 and 2008.

2   Colin Gleadell, 'Artists' colony', *The Telegraph*, 19 October 2001; available online at www.telegraph.co.uk

3   *ARK* Vol.10, 1954, p.15.

4   Rozanne Pibworth, 'Man to Man', *MAN and his Clothes*, November 1954, p.16.

5   See Paul Oliver's classic study of the blues, first published in 1960 and drawing from articles in the music magazine: *Blues Fell This Morning: Meaning in the Blues* (Cambridge and New York: Cambridge University Press), 1990; and Paul Jobling, *Man Appeal: Advertising, Modernism and Menswear* (London and New York: Berg), which discusses *MAN and his Clothes*.

6   Created a Peer in 1991, Leonard Cheshire VC, OM, DSO, DFC, was sent to the Pacific as an official British observer when the first atomic bombs were dropped on the Japanese; he was the Founder of Cheshire Homes International, and his second wife was Sue Ryder.

7   Canney was appointed curator of the Newlyn Orion Gallery in 1956 and began broadcasting on radio and television; see www.lissfineart.com/display.php? KT_artists=Michael+Canney

8   The WHI continues to function and to have influence; for example, the first Kaffe Fassett needlepoint design to be marketed in the 1970s was made into a kit by the WHI at the suggestion of *Vogue* magazine and the second Lady Harlech, its then editor. See http://www.crossstitchermagazine.co.uk/page/crossstitch?entry=interview_with_kaffe_fassett (issue 196, 10 January 2008).

9   *The Times*, Monday, March 15, 1948; see www.time.com/time/printout/0,8816,779714,00.html

10 Eleanor Roosevelt, 'May 3, 1951', *My Day*, see www.gwu.edu/~erpapers/myday/

11 www.fuzzycrawler.com/may00files/may00des.html an article about Gail Hendrix, who worked at the Center during the 1970s.

Into a Fugue

1   The archive of Battersea College of Education is held at the London South Bank University, Archon Code 2110.

2   Her influence on the field is memorialised in the naming of the Constance Howard Resource and Research Centre in Textiles at Goldsmiths College.

3   Audrey Walker, correspondence with the author, November 2008.

4   Eirian Short, correspondence with the author, 20 November 2008.

5   Audrey Walker, *op.cit.*

6   Kay Greenlees, *Creating Sketchbooks for Embroiderers and Textile Artists*, (London: Batsford), 2005, p.60.

7   James Hunting, correspondence with the author, 25 October 2008. See also www.jameshunting.com

8   Alfred Harbage (ed.), *William Shakespeare: the complete works*, revised edition (Baltimore: Penguin Books Inc), 1969, 'King Lear': Act V, Scene 3.

9   *Ibid.*, 'The Tempest': Act IV, Scene 1, starting at line 148.

A Dark Line Runs Through It

1   Su Duncombe Bull, correspondence with the author, November 2008, on her experience of Rozanne as a tutor on the BA Embroidery/Textiles (Hons) course at Goldsmiths, completed in 1985.

2   Eirian Short, correspondence with the author, 20 November 2008.

3   Victoria Brown, correspondence with the author, 18 November 2008. Rozanne arranged an internship with the felt makers, Bury Cooper Whitehead Ltd., for Victoria, and herself designed a series of coats made from naturally-coloured woollen felts, including one with bright, 'Bavarian' embroidery and tassels. The company fascinated her, because it made every grade from the thinnest of felt to metre-thick pads for the brakes of Concord.

4   Penny Lucas, correspondence with Rozanne Hawksley, 22 July 2008.

5   *op.cit.*

6   Kay Greenlees, *Creating Sketchbooks for Embroiderers and Textile Artists*, (London: Batsford), 2005, p.60.

7   Rozanne Pibworth-Hawksley, 'Marks of Significance: A mitre for the Bishop of London', in *The World of Embroidery*, Vol.50, no.2, March 1999, pp.91–2. The mitre was completed in 1998 and is also discussed in Chapter Two.

8   Gold-claret is made of three silk threads, two red and one yellow, which are overlain with strands of gold and red metal (respectively) and then twisted together to form the finished embroidery thread.

9   The Rt Revd.& Rt Hon. Richard Chartres, Bishop of London, correspondence with Rozanne Hawksley, 2 September 1998.

10 Philip Hughes, *Aspects of Narrative in Contemporary Art Textiles in Wales* (The Gallery, Ruthin Craft Centre), 2003, p.25.

11 Andrew Salmon, telephone interview with the author, 10 December 2008.

12 Roger Fry, 'The Artist's Vision', *Vision and Design* (London: Penguin Books), 1961, pp.45–7, the essay first appearing in the *Athenaeum*, in 1919.

13 Oscar Wilde, *De Profundis (The Project Gutenberg Ebook de Profundis)*, transcribed from the 1913 Methuen & Co. edition by David Price, April 13, 2007 [eBook #921].

The Human Condition

1   Michaela Crimmin, 'Art in the danger zone', *RSA Journal*, Spring 2008, p.36.

2   Brian Keenan, *An Evil Cradling*, (London: Vintage Edition published by Arrow, Random House), 1993, p.68.

3   Maggie Grey, 'Editorial', *The World of Embroidery*, Vol.48, no.5, September 1997.

4   Andrew Salmon, Creative Exhibitions' Knitting and Stitching Show press release, August 2000.

5   Canon Terry Palmer, 'Out of the question: Veiled pulpit crucifix', *Church Times*, issue 7536, 17 August 2007, see www.churchtimes.co.uk/content.asp?id=43191

7   www.vam.ac.uk/vastatic/microsites/photography/photographerframe.php?photographerid=ph041

8   Crimmin, *op.cit*, p.36, incorporating the writing of John Berger, in *The Shape of a Pocket*, in an article about David Cotterell's RSA residency in Kabul.

9   Melanie Miller and June Hill, *Mechanical Drawing: the schiffli project* (Manchester Metropolitan University: The Righton Press), 2007, p.43. The exhibition toured the UK for a year from November 2007.

10 Herbert Asquith, *Nightfall*, 1917.

Horrible Truths

1   Jac Scott, *Textile Perspectives in Mixed-Media Sculpture* (Ramsbury: The Crowood Press), 2003, p.136.

2   Alex Seago, *Burning the Box of Beautiful Things: The development of a postmodern sensibility* (Oxford: Oxford University Press), 1995, p.24. The focus of this volume is the RCA's School of Graphic Design.

3   Mathew was born 28 September 1957 and died 8 January 1995.

4   Donne, John and E. K. Chambers (ed.), *Poems of John Donne* vol. I (London: Lawrence & Bullen), 1896, 4–5. Donne, 1572–1631, is thought to have written *Song* prior to 1615, when he converted from Catholicism to the Anglican church and became a priest; most of his works were not published until after his death, in 1633.

5   Scott, *op.cit.*, p.138.

6   *Ibid.*

7   For an analysis of the legislative attempts to introduce both rights-based and role-based equalities for Chilean women, see Merike H. Blofeld and Liesl Haas, 'Defining a Democracy: Reforming the Laws on Women's Rights in Chile, 1990–2002', *Latin American Politics and Society*, Fall 2005, see http://findarticles.com/p/articles/mi_qa4000/is_200510/ai_n15640747

8 Janis Jefferies, telephone interview with the author,
   11 December 2008. The MA existed until 2006, when
   it was absorbed into Art Practices. Rozanne is one of eight
   artists associated with the Goldsmiths' textile course who
   have been interviewed for the NEVAC DVD set, *Narrative
   Threads*, a collaboration between Goldsmiths and the
   University of West England, Bristol, 2006.

9 Carole Murphy, correspondence with Rozanne Hawksley,
   October 2008. Carole is a practicing psychotherapist who
   was a student at the London College of Fashion in the
   1980s and is currently completing a degree with Opus
   School of Textile Arts.

10 Audrey Walker, correspondence with the author,
   November 2008.

11 Jane Wildgoose, correspondence with the author,
   14 December 2008. Jane Wildgoose is an artist, writer,
   and NESTA Dream Time Fellow; and founder of The
   Wildgoose Memorial Library, an ongoing accumulation
   of reference material and a place for meditation and
   consultation on universal themes of life and death.

12 Lizzie was Rozanne's great aunt, a sister of Alice Hunter.

13 *Bonaventure Hammer and John James Burke, Mary, Help
   of Christians: And the Fourteen Saints Invoked as Holy
   Helpers: Instructions, Legends, Novenas and Prayers: with
   Thoughts of the Saints for Every Day in the Year* (New
   York: Benziger Brothers), 1909, p.272.

A Kind of Peace

1 Daniel Miller, *The Comfort of Things* (Cambridge: Polity
   Press), 2008, p.6.

2 For further information see Jule Bunting, 'Take a look at:
   Maidens' Garlands and Memorials', *The Peak Advertiser*,
   25 June 2001, p.13: www.genuki.org.uk/big/eng/DBY/
   TakeaLook/Crantz.html

3 Pennina Barnett, 'Peace and Protest in Britain', *The
   Subversive Stitch,* (Manchester: Whitworth Art Gallery and
   Cornerhouse) 1988, p.50. The exhibition followed on from
   a 1984 book of the same title, by Rozsika Parker. Further
   information also obtained by telephone interview with
   Pennina Barnett, 16 December 2008.

4 Rozanne Hawksley, notes written from her London address
   to Pennina Barnett. The use of gloves in Stuart Brisley's
   work, exhibited March 1983 and entitled '1=66,666' was
   to a degree prompted by Rozanne's explorations around
   gloves in this period.

5 Rozsika Parker, 'Foreword', *The Subversive Stitch, op.cit,* p.5.

6 Nigel Hurlstone, Programme Leader BA Hons Embroidery,
   Manchester Metropolitan University, telephone interview
   with the author, December 2007.

7 John McEwen, 'Friendly, roly-poly and humane', *The
   Sunday Telegraph*, 31 January 1993, Arts section. *Pale
   Armistice* was also included in an amended exhibition
   entitled *No More Heroes Anymore: Contemporary Art from
   the Collection of the Imperial War Museum*, shown at the
   Royal Scottish Academy 11 August to 12 September 1993
   (for which it was the private view card's image).

8 James Hall, 'A small step for man', *The Independent*,
   12 January 1993, p.14, Arts.

9 *Pale Armistice* was again in a selection from their
   contemporary collection, held at the Imperial War
   Museum itself, 13 July – 26 August 1996. Out again for
   the IWM's *The First World War Remembered* (September
   1998 – January 1999), thereafter it remained on show in
   the museum's Atrium displays until it's appearance in their
   exhibition, *Women and War* (15 October 2003 – 18 April
   2004). Sixteen months later it was lent to the Pump House
   Gallery, London for *Ceremony* (10 August – 12 October
   2005), was returned to an Atrium display and then went
   on to *Witness – Highlights from the Art Collection* at the
   IWM North in Manchester (4 February – 23 April 2006).
   Currently it is in the IWM London exhibition, *In
   Memoriam* (30 September 2008 – 9 September 2009).

   The piece was originally commissioned for the Imperial
   War Museum contemporary art collection by Angela
   Weight (Keeper, Department of Art, Imperial War
   Museum 1981–2005).

10 Adrian Ryan, 'Why I paint fish', 1994, from
   www.adrianryan.co.uk/thoughts.htm where can also
   be found an extract from Patrick Heron's *New Statesman*
   review of Ryan's 1948 exhibition at the Redfern Gallery,
   from which the first citation is taken. Ryan taught part-
   time at Goldsmiths from 1947–1983.

11 Illustrated in *Death*, (Cambridge: Cambridge Darkroom
   and Kettle's Yard), 1988, p.33.

12 Stephen Calloway, *Baroque Baroque: the culture of excess*
   (London: Phaidon Press), 1994 (paperback edition 2000),
   p.232.

13 Susan Moore, 'Subversive stitching', *The Financial Times*,
   25 September 1992, Arts section (on *Out of the Frame*
   at the Crafts Council Gallery), and the leaflet for *Box*,
   Walsall Museum and Art Gallery, 17 December 1994
   – 29 January 1995.

14 Rozanne Hawksley, 'The Road to Damascus: An artist's
   journey', *The World of Embroidery*, Vol.48, no.4, July
   1997, p.194.

15 June Hill, extract from 'Sense and Sensibility', a paper
   prepared for and presented at the conference *Memory
   and Touch*, organised by the University College for the
   Creative Arts at the Royal Institute for British Architects,
   7 May 2008.

16 Caiaphas was the high priest who condemned Jesus;
   see William Blake, 'The Everlasting Gospel' in Nicholson
   and Lee (eds.), *The Oxford Book of English Mystical Verse*
   (Oxford: Oxford University Press), 1917, no.58:

   THE VISION OF CHRIST that thou dost see
   Is my vision's greatest enemy.
   Thine has a great hook nose like thine;
   Mine has a snub nose like to mine
   Thine is the Friend of all Mankind;
   Mine speaks in parables to the blind.
   Thine loves the same world that mine hates;
   Thy heaven doors are my hell gates.
   Socrates taught what Meletus
   Loath'd as a nation's bitterest curse
   And Caiaphas was in his own mind
   A benefactor to mankind.
   Both read the Bible day and night,
   But thou read'st black where I read white.

17 Alan Bennett, *Forty Years On* (London: Faber and Faber)
   1969 Act 2, p.77 and Act 1, p.48. By kind permission
   of the author.

Preface

1 Amended from 'Allegorical Odysseys' P Hughes p.36
   Re-Imaging Wales: A Yearbook of the Visual Arts (ed.)
   Hugh Adams, Seren Publications, Cardiff, 2006.

Picture Credits

The publishers would like to thank the following sources
for their kind permission to reproduce the photographs
and illustrations in this book:

The British Library
  MAN and his Clothes 66, 75, 76, 77

Creative Exhibitions
  I shall go The Way whence I shall Not Return 58
  From a Jack to a King – Greed 64

Imperial War Museum
  Pale Armistice front, back, 3, 12, 168
  In Memorium 22, 40
  The Seamstress and the Sea 23

Miles Meehan Gallery
  The Colour Orange – a line of hope 130, 131

Royal College of Art Library, Special Collections
  Rozanne and Brian Aldridge in *Tom Thumb* 71
  Rozanne in *The Beggar's Opera* 72

The Ambassador Publishing Co Ltd
  ARK 10 68

Granada Publishing Ltd
  Pattern Cutting for Beginners 74

J Walter Thompson
  Kellogg's Special K 78

Centurion Publishing Ltd
  Legion magazine 171

Worshipful Company of Weavers
  Mitre for the Bishop of London 18–19, 60, 63

Mission Gallery and Nicola O'Neill
  '...a treaty will be signed sometime today' 08, 134

Every effort has been made to seek permission to reproduce
these images. We are grateful to the individuals and
institutions who have assisted us in this task. Any omissions
are entirely unintentional and details should be addressed
to Ruthin Craft Centre.

Index

CONTRIBUTORS

THE AUTHOR

Mary Schoeser is an internationally renowned
writer and critic, and the author of a series
of influential publications on the applied arts.
Among her many books are *More is More:
an antidote to minimalism*, published in 2001
by Conran Octopus (London) and Reed Publishing
(NZ) Limited; *World Textiles: A Concise History*
(Thames & Hudson 2003); *Silk* (Yale University
Press 2007) and a monograph on *Norma
Starszakowna* (Telos 2005). She is a Senior
Research Fellow at the University of the Arts
London, as well as a freelance writer and curator
who specialises in textiles and wallpaper. Her
most recent exhibition is *A Passion for Painting
Pattern: The textile designs of Raymond Honeyman*,
which is currently touring the UK.

FOREWORD

Dr Ruth Richardson is a historian, writer and
broadcaster in the history of anatomy, architecture,
and illustration. She has lectured and published
widely, and has been a regular columnist in the
medical journal The Lancet. She has co-edited
two books on Medical Humanities for the Royal
College of Physicians, London, but is probably
best known for *Death, Dissection & the Destitute*
(Chicago University Press 2000) and *Vintage Papers
from The Lancet* (Elsevier 2006). She is a Fellow
of the Royal Historical Society, an Affiliated
Scholar in the History & Philosophy of Science at
Cambridge, and Visiting Professor in Humanities,
Hong Kong University. Her most recent book,
The Making of Mr Gray's Anatomy, has been
published by Oxford University Press (2008).

EXHIBITION CURATOR

June Hill is a freelance curator and writer who
practices within the field of textiles. Recent projects
include two Arts Council England funded touring
exhibitions: *Mechanical Drawing – the schiffli
project* (a Manchester Metropolitan University
initiative developed with Dr Melanie Miller)
and *Sow:Sew – New work by Jeanette Appleton*
(developed with the University of Huddersfield).
She writes regularly for *Embroidery* magazine
and is a contributor to Berg's *Encyclopedia
of World Dress and Fashion* (published 2010).

Maiden's Garland, 2009.

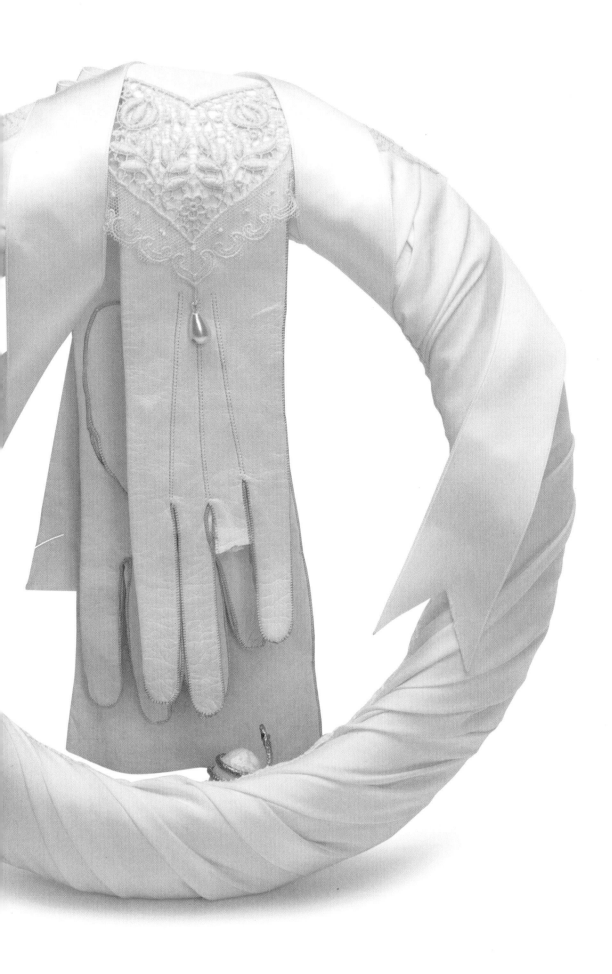

Acknowledgments

The Artist

For his kind permission to use passages from *Forty Years On*, I would like to thank Alan Bennett. My thanks and gratitude also go to Mary Schoeser for the manner in which she has turned seeming chaos into a truthful line, and to the wise June Hill, patient minder and curator. I would like to express deep gratitude to Philip Hughes, Dewi Tannatt Lloyd and Lisa Rostron for enabling my work to be so sympathetically documented and shown. I would also like to express my grateful thanks to everyone I have known for making my life what it was and is. Thanks also for the grant scholarship system that enabled me to go to art school and college.

The Artist and Author

For their recollections and permission to quote from correspondence with the artist and the author, thanks go to Pennina Barnett, Victoria Brown, Su Duncombe Bull, The Rt Rev & Rt Hon Richard Chartres, James Hunting, Nigel Hurlstone, Janis Jefferies, Penny Lucas, Carole Murphy, Elizabeth Price, Andrew Salmon, Eirian Short, Frankie Slater, Audrey Walker and Jane Wildgoose. For their help in obtaining information and photographs, the author wishes to acknowledge the assistance of Angela Godwin (Director of Public Services, Imperial War Museum), Jo Hall (Editor, *Embroidery* magazine), Neil Parkinson (Special Collections Manager, Royal College of Art Library), Jane Phillips (Director, Mission Gallery), Nicola O'Neill, Andrew Salmon (Director, Creative Exhibitions) and Jenny Wood (Senior Curator, Department of Art, Imperial War Museum). For their kindness while crammed together on a transatlantic flight, the author thanks Mr and Mrs Fairweather, and for professional courtesies while transiting the US, Lynn Felsher (Curator of Textiles, The Museum at FIT) and Dilys Blum (Senior Curator of Costume and Textiles, Philadelphia Museum of Art).

This volume would not have been possible without the support of Philip Hughes, Director, Ruthin Craft Centre, and Deputy Director, Jane Gerrard. Painstaking editing was undertaken by June Hill, also curator of the exhibition this book accompanies. Dr Ruth Richardson provided an invaluable additional insight through her foreword, while Lisa Rostron and the team at Lawn, Dylan Chubb, Stephen Heaton and Aled Brown, have worked with sensitivity and patient dedication in its design and production.

We would particularly like to thank the photographers who have made possible this permanent record of the artist's work. Images taken by Dil Bannerjee, Philip Clarke, Adrian Flowers, Clifford Hatts, Brian Hawksley, Rob Kennard, the Myles Meehan Gallery, Bob Pullen, Nicola O'Neill, Mike Sage and Denys Short are identified as such in the captions. The remainder are the work of Dewi Tannatt Lloyd.

The Publishers

Ruthin Craft Centre would like to thank: Rozanne Hawksley, June Hill, Mary Schoeser, Ruth Richardson, Dewi Tannatt Lloyd, Lisa Rostron, Stephen Heaton, Dylan Chubb, Aled Brown, Lucy Clark; Moira Stevenson, Graham Holland, Andrew Salmon, Audrey Walker, Nicola O'Neill, Pete Manford, The Rt Rev & Rt Hon Richard Chartres, Janet Laws, Lynn Szygenda, the Embroiderers' Guild, Deborah Richards, Jane Phillips, Sarah James, Tod Grimwade; Hafina Clwyd, Greg Parsons, Einir Wyn Jones, Olga Byrne, Roger Mansbridge, Gwawr Jones, Sarah Dolan; Sandra Bosanquet, Roger Lefevre, Ceri Jones, Gwenno Jones; Wales Arts International and the Arts Council of Wales, Pete Goodridge and ArtWorks.

Dedication

For our bringers of love and happiness: Terry, Mathew, Brian, and Barney 'the noodle' Johnson.